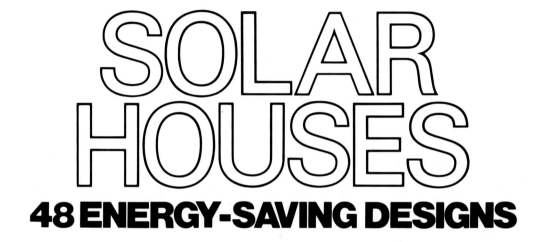

SOLAR HOUSES
48 ENERGY-SAVING DESIGNS

For my wife, Jane,
our daughters, Amy and Lauren,
and our children's children.

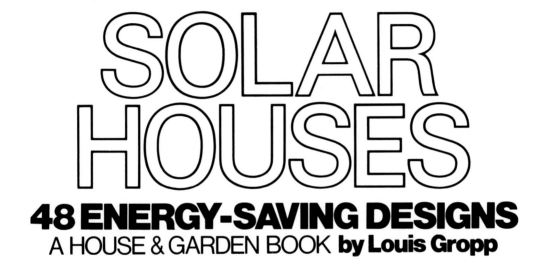

SOLAR HOUSES

48 ENERGY-SAVING DESIGNS
A HOUSE & GARDEN BOOK by Louis Gropp

Pantheon Books·New York

Copyright ©1978 by The Condé Nast Publications Inc.
Photographs Copyright ©1973, 1974, 1975, 1976, 1977, 1978 by
The Condé Nast Publications Inc.

All rights reserved under International and Pan-American Copyright Conventions. Published in the United States by Pantheon
Books, a division of Random House, Inc., New York, and simulta-
neously in Canada by Random House of Canada Limited,
Toronto.

Library of Congress Cataloging in Publication Data

Gropp, Louis.
    Solar Houses.

    "A House & Garden Book."
    Bibliography: p. 159
    Includes index.
    1. Solar Houses — Design and construction.   I. Title.
TH7414.G76   697'.78   78-51802

Manufactured in United States of America   98765

ISBN 0-394-50089-X
ISBN 0-394-73543-9 pbk.

Contents

Acknowledgments

The author of this book owes a great debt to the editors, writers, artists, and photographers who work together to produce *House & Garden* and the *House & Garden Guides,* where plans for most of the houses that make up the body of this book were first published. This book would have been impossible without them, and I want them all to know how much I appreciate their contribution to the book, as well as working with them at the Condé Nast Publications Inc., as editor-in-chief of the *House & Garden Guides.* Special thanks must go to Albert Hamowy, who designed this book, to Carol Knobloch, who did the art production and to Gere Gallagher, my editorial assistant. I want to thank William Rayner, the editorial business manager at Condé Nast, for his support; and Paul Bonner, director of the Condé Nast book division. I also appreciate the early interest and support of Barbara Plumb, my editor at Pantheon, and Connie Mellon, my production editor there. And I am grateful for the original work done by Elizabeth Sverbeyeff Byron, trends and environments editor, and Will Mehlhorn, architectural editor, of *House & Garden.* Photographs are always the raw material of a book on architecture, and I owe special thanks to the photographers who gave this book its unique visual quality and who frequently introduced me, through their lenses, to the houses that follow. Which brings me to the most important contributors of all: the homeowners who have been willing to share their houses with us, and the architects and designers who are creating the new solar architecture. They have my admiration, my respect, and my appreciation for their original contribution to architecture and to the quality of all our lives. May they continue to look up and find the sun.
Louis Gropp

Designer: Albert T. Hamowy

Foreword

From the pioneer log cabin to the great modern sky-scraper, American architecture has responded to the needs of the times. At its best it has been a blend of both practicality and style.

In recent years architecture has been presented with an increasingly important challenge; a challenge arising from the recognition that our fossil energy resources are finite and are rapidly diminishing. The continued development of our nation depends on our ability to conserve energy, to use it more efficiently, and to place greater reliance upon energy from renewable resources.

No longer can we afford the luxury of designing and building our homes, our offices and our factories without fully considering the amount and the type of energy they will consume. No longer can we afford not to factor in energy efficiency and conservation into our planning.

Buildings of all types should increasingly derive much of their energy from the sun, the wind, and other renewable resources. Already solar energy is economical and practical for many applications in many parts of the United States. Homes like those in this book demonstrate that architectural style and elegance need not be sacrificed in order to capture and use solar energy.

Owners, designers and builders today face the challenge, and have the opportunity, to help the nation solve its grave energy problems. Many people, as illustrated in the following pages, can take satisfaction in the knowledge that they already are helping to create a new "fashion" and life-style—that they are in the forefront of a profound and exciting change.

The interest you are showing by reading this publication is symptomatic of a growing energy awareness across America. It is the government's hope that your interest will be translated into action, and to that end we in the Department of Energy will provide all the support we can muster.

James R. Schlesinger
Secretary of Energy

Introduction

This book is a compilation — a celebration, really — of the houses that are being built as a result of the nationwide quest for a solution to our energy problems. There are now thirty to forty thousand houses in the United States that get at least some of their heat from the sun. Five years ago there were only two hundred or so. By 1985 the federal government hopes the number of solar houses will have increased to 2.5 million, and studies by the National Science Foundation project 4.4 million solar buildings by the year 2000.

Surveying the staggering potential of solar energy, *Fortune* magazine speculated that power from the sun could become the "biggest economic development since the automobile." And in late 1977, the *New York Times* reported that solar energy development "is progressing faster than either Washington or its advocates expected."

Thanks to the spreading impetus of favorable legislation in many states and the aid and loan benefits already accepted by the congressional conferees working on President Carter's initial energy bill, the late 1970s will mark the transition to a post-petroleum era, a turning point in the development of a new solar architecture.

What will these new solar houses look like? How will they function? What will solar energy systems do to the cost of building a house and the way in which we live in it?

The answers to these questions can be found in the growing number of houses that use solar energy for a significant portion of their heat. The economics and aesthetics of solar housing are being resolved right now, all around us, before our eyes, in our time.

The object of any type of solar heat system is to catch and accumulate enough of the dispersed energy of the sun to provide useful heat and to store enough of it to last through nights and cloudy days.

Two kinds of solar energy systems — one known as passive, the other as active — have been developed to do this. The passive systems use the house itself — its windows, walls, and interior spaces — to collect, store, and distribute the heat from the sun. The active systems turn to more mechanical means, hardware, like the flat-plate collectors seen on solar house roofs, to collect the sun's heat and distribute it throughout the house or send it to storage for later use as required.

Every day the sun bombards the earth with several thousand times as much energy as we consume. The solar energy reaching the earth every three days is greater than the estimated total of all the fossil fuels on earth. In fact, the solar energy annually striking the roof of a typical house is said to be ten times as great as its annual heat demand.

Solar heating systems, properly designed and integrated to use this heat efficiently, can provide a large percentage of a house's space heating and domestic hot water requirements. Technically, it is possible to achieve close to 100 percent solar heating and cooling; however, a more realistic and economically feasible goal would be 70 percent solar space heating and 90 percent solar hot water heating.

Up until fairly recently, the conventional wisdom was that there were few economic incentives for the use of solar energy. More traditional energy sources — natural gas, oil and coal, or electricity, which is generated almost exclusively by the burning of these fossil fuels — had been relatively cheap and available. As a result, buildings were designed automatically to be dependent on fossil fuels for heating space and domestic hot water. The same fuels powered the systems that provided for other modern-day comforts — like climate conditioning and electronic conveniences.

But all that changed with the energy crisis of 1973. Utility bills jumped 48 percent and heating fuel costs shot up 68.3 percent between 1973 and 1975. And it is generally agreed now that energy costs have nowhere to go but up. With the rising costs of conventional energy came renewed interest in the "free" energy provided by the sun.

Solar energy *is* free and dependable. But the systems that collect, store, and distribute the heat from the sun cost money. For that reason, the economic decision of whether to use the sun's energy or the alternative, fossil fuel, had always been made by comparing the cost of a solar system and possible backup with the cost of conventional heating systems and the fuel they require. Until recently, the latter won hands down.

But the latter involved nonrenewable resources, and so the balance was inevitably tipping in favor of the sun — abundant, free, and nonpolluting. The tip point came in late 1976, when a study found solar energy had become competitive with conventional energy in thirteen cities around the country (see Solar Economics, page 149).

In most cases the first costs of a solar system will be much higher than the cost of a conventional heating system; and solar systems almost always require a backup conventional system in any case. However, when looked at over the lifetime of the system, the solar systems, in total, are sometimes less expensive than conventional heating alone because of the accumulated savings in fuel costs.

It should be pointed out that with passive solar design, first costs are very minimal, as the solar collecting, storage, and distribution functions are usually carried by building elements that would be part of a good house design anyway. With active systems, more specific solar hardware is involved, and the hardware does cost money.

The design and size of the house, climatic conditions, and the size and type of the desired system all figure in the amount you might spend for solar energy. In the 1976 federal government solar demonstration program, combined solar heating and hot water systems for single-family houses ranged in cost from $5,000 to $19,000. The cost for domestic hot water only was about $1,500 to $2,500. Uninstalled, a domestic hot water system can cost from $800 to $1,500.

Although many still refuse to believe that the energy crisis is real, the fact is that traditional forms of energy are running out. The lines at the gas stations may come and go, but the gas and oil underground decrease with each passing year.

The U.S. Department of Energy points out that the production of fuel will peak in 1990 and then diminish through the year 2050, when we will have depleted our oil resources. Meanwhile, Americans, 6 percent of the world's population, use 36 percent of the world's energy.

But this, too, is changing. Even as the number of people throughout the world continues to grow, so do their expectations. Energy requirements, here, there, and everywhere, are escalating—for as E.F. Schumacher said in his book *Small Is Beautiful:* "Energy is for the mechanical world what consciousness is for the human world." And we have devised a very energy-dependent mechanical world.

From the perspective of an advanced energy systems manager, "It's a hard fact of life, but every time OPEC [Organization of Petroleum Exporting Countries] acts to increase petroleum prices, every time a local utility raises its rate, or every time an energy shortage occurs, the prospects for solar energy systems improve."

The reason is simple. Our society is using up our favorite nonrenewable fossil fuels—oil and natural gas—at a furious pace. We do have large coal reserves, but learning to use them without damage to our environment will take time. (The shift by electric utilities to dirtier fuels—particularly coal—has canceled out any improvements that power companies have made in controlling pollution in recent years, according to a report by the Council of Economic Priorities. In a 430-page study, the New York-based environmental group concludes that "the rapid shift to coal as the primary fossil energy source for electrical generation is likely to delay, and in some cases prevent, the achievement of air quality goals.") And for all of us, the stuff

of nuclear energy—both fuels and wastes—present substantial problems of their own.

"The energy crisis is not going to disappear," wrote Rodney and Sydney Wright in *Inland Architecture* (April 1977), in an article defining the new stance of their now solar-oriented architectural practice in Chicago. "We are at the beginning of the new solar age—the end of the fossil fuel age," they continued. "Health and hazard problems surround both coal and nuclear development. Solar is safe on your roof."

"For anyone using solar energy, looking for the sun is going to be first on each day's agenda," says solar architect Bruce Anderson. "Such a person is also going to go to great lengths to utilize the sun's energy as wisely as possible. Out of solar heating comes energy conservation."

With growing awareness of a very real energy crisis, the federal government is now acting to stimulate energy conservation, and government financing of solar development has also accelerated significantly. In fiscal year 1978, the government will spend a record $368 million on solar research, development, and demonstration, and the subsidy will be even larger if Congress goes along with President Carter's plan to allow tax credits for people investing in solar heating equipment and energy-conservation measures.

Some sense the beginning of a shift in what they have seen as the "high-cost, high-technology approach" advocated by government agencies such as ERDA [The Energy Research and Development Administration], FEA [Federal Energy Administration], both now included in DOE [Department of Energy], and HUD [Department of Housing and Urban Development], and reflected in many of the costly solar heating products offered by the new solar industry.

One sign of this shift is that, increasingly, the government is working with the architectural profession to reorient architects to their history of solar building.

A survey of architects by the American Institute of Architects/Research Corporation (for the National Science Foundation) revealed that there were no insurmountable problems to using solar heating and cooling in the built environment. Rather, the report emphasized that the problems that did exist had as much to do with architectural expertise as with solar technology.

Most encouraging is the growing feeling being expressed within the architectural profession that the real answer to capturing the energy of the sun will be found in the design of buildings, as much as in adding solar hardware to them.

The energy-conscious houses shown in the following pages illustrate both active and passive solutions to solar building. They cover a broad spectrum geographically, economically, and technologically. Their addresses range from San Diego, California, to Quechee, Vermont; from Portland, Oregon, to Fort Lauderdale, Florida. Their building budgets are as far ranging as their zip codes: from under $10,000 build-it-yourself examples to sophisticated designs well over $100,000, and everywhere in between. Price has no relationship to ingenuity. Tight budgets can lead to some of the best-integrated solar architectural designs; large budgets can float some grand experiments, too. The choice of an active or passive system is an equally poor criteria for determining the best solar designs. Some of the most efficient solutions are hybrids combining elements of both.

In this book are custom-designed houses by well-known architects and others by architects who have yet to become widely known for their contributions to solar building. There are houses you can order through a manufacturer, with solar hardware as part of the package, and plans of house designs that you can buy and contract to have built using "off-the-shelf" solar hardware.

Examples were not chosen because they seemed the perfect solar house, but rather because they represented the best possible total living environment. They had to be places in which people would like to live. They had to be good architecture. They had to be houses where climatic responses were as important to the overall design as the more traditional criteria of function and imagery. As architect Bruce Anderson has said, "A built environment indiscriminately placed in the natural environment becomes ugly, no matter how 'elegant' the forms, or how 'rich' the materials, or how 'tasteful' and 'stylish' the lines."

Even a short time ago, most professionals dealing with architecture and building in one way or another did not seem to recognize this. Architectural critic Ada Louise Huxtable wrote recently in the *New York Times*, "The 'truth' about it [art, including architecture] shifts with the calendar, and its coloration with every season of the mind. Vision depends on a moment in time. A different message is delivered for each generation." Or in the words of the hymn by James Russell Lowell, "New occasions bring new duties; Time makes ancient goods uncouth."

This generation may be coming to understand that the answer to our residential energy problems may be shining overhead, there since the fourth day of creation. From that understanding is evolving a new kind of house, where the sun, not fossil fuels, supplies the energy.

This is a book about houses being designed for a new era, the post-petroleum era, when energy matters. "With the energy crisis as catalyst, a new architectural revolution has begun," says San Diego architect Rob Wellington Quigley. "We must articulate a new environmental architecture directly responsible to the climate in which it exists. This new, and necessarily regional, aesthetic will evolve by integrating the common sense of primitive and 'pre-cheap-energy' buildings, new solar high-tech and low-tech engineering innovations, and the economic realities of current construction practices." Unfortunately, "a conflict between the general feeling that 'beauty is what you're used to,' and the reality that what we're used to is irresponsible design, is the present state of the art," he says.

This "state of the art" is a product of technology developed over the past fifty years, according to a new book by New York City architect Richard G. Stein. As mechanical engineers produced reliable central heating and ventilating systems, architects could treat their buildings as pure, isolated forms. Fans and furnaces could do what wind and sun had done before. But "our building history is a history of solar architecture," he points out, with building shapes, sites and materials chosen to take advantage of sun, shade, and breeze.

Essentially this is a description of passive solar house design, where the structure itself acts as the collector of the sun's energy, its materials are chosen to store the sun's heat, and its spaces designed to distribute that heat as it is needed.

A growing number of solar advocates feel that the passive approach is *the* approach to solar house design. Architect Travis Price wrote in *Popular Science:* "The right approach is to do it as simply as possible, letting nature work to keep a house comfortable, and using simple, existing building materials and techniques. I think that future architecture will, as much as possible, heat and cool itself independently of outside energy sources. If you work with the environment and off-the-shelf hardware, you can build homes that are livable, attractive, affordable and low in energy consumption."

Price's conviction that you don't need sophisticated, expensive, high-technology equipment to conserve energy and utilize the sun's heat is shared by many pioneers in solar energy for residential application. One of their leading spokesmen is inventor Steve Baer of Zomeworks, in Albuquerque, New Mexico, who advocates low-technology passive systems. "South-facing windows are actually solar collectors," Steve Baer points out, "and if you can prevent them from losing heat at night, they can become very efficient." Several of the products coming out of Zomeworks are Baer's attempt to do just that, as the houses to come will illustrate.

Within active systems there are also varying degrees of high- and low-tech approaches. The water-trickling collector developed by Harry Thomason is a good example of a low-tech active system; those involving photovoltaic cells, electronic control systems, computers, and miniaturization are more aligned to the high-technology world of NASA life-support systems—all of which have enhanced the movement toward a solar future.

There are many other encouraging solar signals:

Architects from New York City to San Diego are now talking about the urgent need to relearn the way to build buildings simply and without a complete surrender to energy-dependent systems.

More of the federal energy research money is going into the study of regional climatic conditions, the possibilities of integrated passive solar design, and consumer information.

Growing numbers of people are becoming intrigued with the idea of energy self-sufficiency, of creating an energy system capable of meeting the needs of their children and their children's children.

And across the country, solar houses are being built with collectors smiling on their roofs, the sun's warmth is being collected inside water tanks and thermal walls, and the people inside are basking in the free, clean rays of the sun and sensing anew its power and energy and their participation in one of nature's greatest wonders.

This book then becomes a celebration of a new generation of solar houses that give evidence that we may now be ready for the sun's "truth" or "message" to us: that within it is the energy to fulfill that charge to every generation—to replenish the earth.

Passive
solar systems

Passive solar systems collect solar heat, store and deliver it, in the most elegant examples, without any hardware driven by energy-hungry machinery. Following this introduction to passive systems we will show a wide variety of passive solar houses. Although their solar systems, once resolved, are often simplicity itself, behind them is a great deal of ingenuity, for what is demanded in passive solar house design is a highly sophisticated understanding of the nature of heat.

In a passive solar house, the building—its orientation to the sun, its use and placement of glass, its other material choices — becomes the system. Heat storage is usually integral to the structure itself — adobe, brick, or concrete walls, sometimes covered with glass, collect, trap, and radiate the heat. Drumwalls or other containers provide alternative means for collecting, storing, and radiating the heat of the sun. Insulating and reflecting panels, plus forms of ventilation, improve the performance of these systems and increase their efficiency. Because all of this is little more than a few unusual uses of standard, available materials, passive systems afford construction economies. They are built of materials that can be easily obtained; they can be installed by local contractors without any specialized solar training; they are often building elements that would be a part of any good house, solar or not. The devices used in passive systems can be as simple as a window or a greenhouse; as ingenious as a drumwall or self-regulating Skylid; or as high-sounding as "thermosyphoning," which is the term that, simply put, describes heat's natural tendency to rise.

Because passive solar collection does use the entire building or various elements of it—e.g., walls, roofs, openings—as solar components, the collector and the building are one and the same element and cannot be separated from each other. (Active solar collectors, on the other hand, which will

be discussed and demonstrated in a following section, are relatively independent elements that can be organized and operated quite apart from the building itself.) The integrated nature of passive solar collection, as the designs that follow will demonstrate, permits an amazing variation in house design — as the designs are conceived in response to the conditions of their microclimate, an authentic regional architecture is the unselfconscious result.

Like most, the passive solar houses in this book rely on two general passive collector concepts. They are: (1) collection through solar windows, including greenhouses and skylights (known as roof monitors); and (2) building elements, e.g., masonry walls, that combine in themselves the collection, storage, and distribution functions.

Solar Windows

Because they also serve various other purposes—visibility, ventilation, natural illumination — as well as incidental heat collection, windows will be seen as particularly valuable collectors in passive solar designs. The use of south-facing windows to increase heat gain directly into a building is well known. The south-wall orientation is considered ideal compared to east and west walls because in northern climates shading of a south window to prevent summer overheating is easily accomplished by an overhang calculated to equinox sun angles. The winter sun is lower in the sky than the summer sun and will come further into the house if it is invited. When a window is used as a solar collector, insulating the window at night is important, preferably from the interior, or the heat so easily gained will be just as easily lost. With insulating draperies, or interior shutters or panels that can be much more airtight, windows can function as effective heat traps and are able to provide a sizable percentage of the annual heat requirements of a building (estimates vary from 25 to 60 percent, depending on climate and use).

Windows can have the drawback of overheating the space they serve. The solution is to store the unwanted heat for distribution later. Masonry surfaces such as concrete, brick, tile, or stone on the floor or on the walls can be used for their heat-storage capacity, absorbing the heat during the day and radiating it subsequently for several hours or more when the space cools off. The storage effect of a particular floor or wall can be calculated by a solar engineer. Too great a storage effect in the exposed room surfaces can have a negative effect on the comfort of the people using the room or on the fuel consumption required if the morning "reheat" time of the materials is too long. However, properly designed, the thermal mass of construction materials can play a significant role in storing the sun's heat for radiation at a more desirable time.

Solar Greenhouses

Greenhouses are another tool of some of our passive solar houses. The use of a greenhouse as a solar heat trap is an obvious extension of the solar window collector concept. It exposes more glass area to solar radiation than a window, but with greater heat loss if no provision is made for insulation. Double glazing is as important in greenhouses as elsewhere. Two layers of glass are just about twice as effective at keeping heat in as one, with the dead-air space between serving as insulation. Without a second layer of glass, a greenhouse can either chill or overheat a house. (Another solution is the Beadwall, a patented vacuum-driven system by Zomeworks that fills and empties a cavity between two sheets of glass or plastic with polystyrene beads, thus substantially increasing the insulating characteristics of the glass wall.) Storage such as masonry surfaces or a rock pile under the greenhouse is sometimes used to avoid overheating the space.

To make a greenhouse energy efficient it is necessary to be able to control the heat, to hold it for later use, if necessary, rather than to throw it out the vents while the sun is high. There are several fairly simple ways this is done. Drums full of water can soak up daytime heat for release at night when the temperature in the greenhouse falls below the temperature of the drums. Rocks are also used as a heat storage medium: a bin full of them, wire-sided so that warm air can move through them, could support plants and work counters.

For most greenhouses, heat gain is a more pressing problem. The summer sun can be brutal, turning a helpful collector into a solar furnace. Many greenhouse manufacturers are now marketing sliding shades, slatted for summer sun-and-shade effect. Deciduous trees — which grow leaves in summer that provide welcome shade, then shed them in the fall when the sun is desired—help greenhouse sun control even as they do walls of windows. Vines, trained on strings or wire, can fill in until newly planted trees mature. One advantage of the greenhouse as a solar collector is that it can be closed off from the rest of the house on sunless days, thereby reducing the net heated area of the building. And during periods of moderate weather, a greenhouse can be useful as a supplementary living space—as an atrium, a sun room, or garden room.

Solar Roof Monitors

Other versatile passive collectors seen in many of the houses in this book are skylights or clerestory shed arrangements designed to control heat gain, natural light, and/or ventilation. Because with these roof monitors heat enters at the high, i.e., hottest, point of the building, and because the roof exposure gains so much radiation in the summer, shading or insulating arrangements are required. One control device is the Skylid developed by Steve Baer and manufactured by his firm, Zomeworks. The Skylids, composed of louvers placed on the underside of a skylight, automatically open to let the sun in through an ingenious control that requires no electricity. It operates with the help of Freon, a gas that moves back and forth between two canisters according to the heat of the sun, opening the Skylids during sunny weather and closing them during very cloudy periods and at night. A manual override allows the owner to close the shutters entirely in summer. With a return-air register, located at a high point in the space, trapped heat can be recirculated, returning solar heat gained through the building and roof monitors to the lower occupied spaces.

Roof monitors in the houses that follow are excellent sources of natural lighting and can often be used in summer months to augment natural cooling through the "thermal-chimney" effect; the natural rise of hot air in a building can be vented through them to the exterior, causing a continuous circulation of air for ventilating purposes.

Storage

The radiation received from solar windows does increase the temperature of room air and surfaces exposed to the sun's rays. As such, the room's air and exposed surfaces (walls, floors, etc.) become the solar storage area for a window wall, greenhouse, or roof monitor that collects the radiation. For most situations the storage capacity of the air, a brick floor, or masonry wall will not be sufficient for long periods of heating demand, nor offer any exacting controls. In the process of "charging" the storage, the space may become overheated and possibly extremely uncomfortable for the occupants.

Considerable know-how in providing the right amount of storage is important. The room size, the window placement, the material composition, volume and weight, and the expected temperature difference help determine the performance of the solar storage. To effectively use the radiation stored in the air and room surfaces, careful attention must be given to minimizing the loss of heat at night or when collection is not occurring. Insulated draperies, shutters, Beadwalls, and other such devices help reduce heat loss and increase the use of trapped heat in the more successful solar houses.

Building Elements for Collection and Storage

The second set of passive collector concepts illustrated by some of the houses in this edition makes use of heat that is built up within a wall or the roof structure of a building. This is done by syphoning, or drawing off, the heat and supplying it to a room or storage element. "Thermosyphoning," a term traditionally applied to mechanical systems that use the natural rise of heated gases or liquids for heat transport, is the primary method for moving captured heat to point of use or storage. To avoid overheating in the summer, the space where the heat builds up is vented to the exterior.

One thermosyphoning concept uses solar heat trapped in air spaces in walls and roofs. When the temperature of the trapped air exceeds the temperature of the space to be heated, it can be drawn off by direct venting or forced-air duct arrangements. A variation of this concept is one where the wall or roof is transparent. Ducted fiberglass panels are under development for just such an application. Not considered as effective as active flat-plate collectors, they would have the advantage of admitting natural light, and providing better insulation than a plate-glass window.

The Trombe Wall

The building envelope, i.e., its walls, can also be used as storage. A good example of this is the Trombe wall, where glass is placed over an absorbing material — generally masonry — which is painted dark and serves as heat storage for a time-lag capacity that has been previously calculated. The air space between the glass wall and the absorbing material is vented to the interior at the top of the wall or ducted to storage elsewhere in the building. A cold-air return is located at the bottom of the collector wall so that a thermosyphoning arrangement can be used to facilitate air circulation. Insulation is sometimes placed on the room side of the storage wall to avoid overheating the space.

The Drumwall

A variation on storing the sun's energy in an exposed masonry wall is to expose containers filled with water to solar radiation. The water containers may be placed on the roof or used as interior or exterior walls. Again, determining the proper size of the storage capacity is important. The drumwall, developed by Steve Baer, is the clearest example of this storage device. Steel oil drums, filled with water, are stacked in vertical racks on the inside of a glass wall. The drums, painted black on the end that faces the sun, absorb solar heat and then release it into the interior after the sun is down. Space between the drums also admits natural light and the sun's heat directly into the interior, and one can see between the drums to the outside. The direct sunlight into the interior space provides a faster warm-up time in the morning than a solid masonry collector storage wall would, and the water potentially stores more heat than would an equivalent volume of masonry. An outside insulating panel controls overheating in summer and heat loss on winter nights. Manually operated, the insulating panel also serves as a reflector when in the open position.

Reflectors

One way that will be seen to increase heat gain on passive collector devices, as well as on active ones, is to add highly reflective surfaces. Panels with a reflectible surface positioned at an angle designed to take maximum advantage of the sun with respect to the collector increase the amount of solar radiation received by reflecting the sun's rays from an area larger than the collector itself. Simply by changing the position of a reflector once a month, the incident angle of reflected radiation can be improved as the sun changes in altitude throughout the year. Some reflector panels can also be raised to insulate the collector wall when that is preferable; still others act as sunshades for windows below the collector array. All provide a simple method for increasing heat gain.

Passive vs Active Systems

Solar heating with the passive means we include in this book are often ignored by advocates of more technically complex solar heating systems. One obvious reason is economic. Passive systems are design- not product-oriented, and so they do not spin off a new marketable commodity. It is hard to sort out what parts or elements of a passive solar building are there to serve the energy system; in an independent active system it seems more obvious. This can complicate things when talking about grants, too. It may explain why the government stimulation of solar energy housing has leaned heavily on the side of active systems. A descriptive summary of HUD Cycle 3 Solar Residential Projects, published in the summer of 1977, listed 169 projects: 159 of them were for active systems, 6 were hybrids (combining active and passive elements), and only 4 were passive.

There are disadvantages to passive systems: They often mean a wider variation of indoor temperature due to slow warm-up time on cold mornings (which is why most passive solar houses also have stoves) and overheating on extremely sunny days. These disadvantages are being overcome by using insulating devices and fan-controlled heat distribution systems. Some of the passive devices may strike the average homeowner as unconventional, and due to the slow response times of high-thermal-capacity construction, passive systems do impose their own regime on the homeowner who may be used to the more easily controlled, conventional heating system.

Owners of passive solar structures generally do have to be very involved in their houses. They become increasingly sun-conscious and seem to enjoy the new habits required by their active participation with nature: opening and closing vents, skylights, doors, and dampers; adjusting reflectors, pulling draperies, or closing insulating panels; putting on sweaters; lighting wood fires; accepting wider temperature variations, even occasional discomfort. But living closer to the rhythms of nature, looking for the sun, turns out to be a positive, not a negative, aspect of their self-imposed energy-consciousness.

A major advantage of passive systems is the financial one of construction economies. Installing mechanical heating equipment in a building usually proves expensive. As a result, a basic principle of practical energy-conscious house design emerges: to first insulate the house in a way to cut down on energy requirements, to then use passive means of solar energy collecting, storing, and distributing heat to the best possible advantage, in a way that is appropriate for each climate. This kind of energy-conscious design will lighten the load on whatever mechanical heating equipment is chosen, whether it includes an active solar heating component or not.

The passive solar houses on the following forty pages are visually striking in their design ingenuity, producing some of the most interesting forms to come out of the new solar architecture. They demonstrate much better than can ever be said how the integrated nature of passive solar systems permits — perhaps invites — an amazing variety in the design of a house. The imagination of the designer and builder and the openness of the homeowner are the only limiting factors, and from the houses you are about to see, that will seem to be no limitation at all.

Passive solar systems

A house in league with nature

Built and oriented on its site with the sun in mind, this design realizes passive solar premise: "The house itself is the system."

Wise orientation of the building to its site, the overall design of the structure itself, and many of its components all have a share in the way this house works with nature. Standing in rugged foothills near central New Mexico, the stucco house was designed by architect Stephen E. Earnest for the Fred Herzon family to invite the sun in to help do the heating. The architect worked with solar consultant Steve Baer to devise a passive solar system that would be integral to the house itself.

Among the components in the structure's passive solar system are its stucco exterior walls in a dark tone for better heat absorption; reflective white gravel on roofs; and 2-by-6-inch framing that allows for extra insulation. Skylights with adjustable reflectors, brick floors, metal drums painted black and filled with water, and wood-burning stoves in three rooms also have specific jobs to do. Reflective panels over skylights open to let sun in directly when available and desired. Brick pavers throughout and metal drums near windowed areas on the lower level serve as thermal masses: They retain solar heat and radiate its warmth after the sun goes down and room air begins to cool. The stoves, usually lighted only in severely cold evenings, also help keep the house warm until sunup. The three-level house is set on the lower part of a south-facing slope, and setbacks on the south side are largely faced with glass so major rooms get much sunlight. The stepped-up arrangement of rooms also takes advantage of the fact that hot air rises. On the colder north side there are few windows. The sum of all these features works well enough so that standby electric strips are not called upon often.

To cool the house in summer, water flows through boxes in the east and west walls; air drawn from the outside passes over the water and then goes through ducts to the rooms. This evaporative cooling system requires only a small fan in each box and thus uses little electricity. Also, to keep the house cool in summer, on the west, "where summer sun is a long time setting and it is hottest between four and five in the afternoon," according to architect Earnest, there are no windows, only sliding glass doors in the living room and those are shaded by courtyard walls.   [*Continued*]

Glass at all levels and metal drums on lower floor bring solar heat to rooms.

North side has a carport, few windows.   Skylight reflectors increase heat gain.

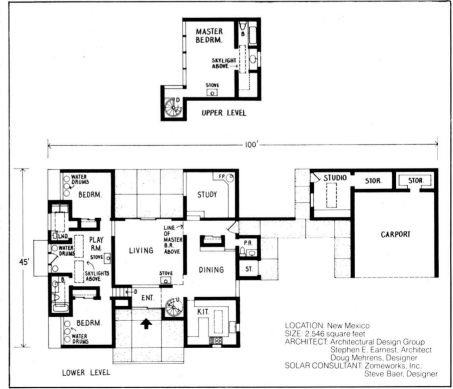

LOCATION: New Mexico
SIZE: 2,546 square feet
ARCHITECT: Architectural Design Group
Stephen E. Earnest, Architect
Doug Mehrens, Designer
SOLAR CONSULTANT: Zomeworks, Inc.
Steve Baer, Designer

GLEN ALLISON

16

The sun does its part so quietly in the Herzon house that the family can "hear nature —birds and crickets and coyotes—instead of furnace noises," says Dr. Herzon. "The house responds to the environment, to its variations in temperature, so we are always sensitive to what is happening outside." The Herzons find that living with nature has economic advantages as well as aesthetic pleasures. Under state laws that encourage the use of solar energy in houses, Dr. Herzon received a tax credit for specific solar-related components. And in the first year the family lived in their new house, consumption of electricity for all purposes, including heating and cooling, was about half of that estimated for an equal-size structure without solar energy. Besides the energy-saving system, the house incorporates other features that Fred and Sandy Herzon sought: a handsome design at home in the natural landscape; well-separated areas for themselves and their two young sons, and an isolated art studio for Mrs. Herzon, a sculptor.

In bedroom: fourposter, wood stove.

In study: a fireplace to warm the soul.

Mirrors flank scenic view over lavatory.

Clerestories stretch along the south wall of the living room, opposite top. Almost house-wide, the room can be swept by breezes: On the east it has a large wall opening with sliding glass doors beyond; on the west are sliding glass doors that open directly to a sheltered court. Over dining table, opposite bottom, operating-room lights serve as a chandelier. Walls are painted gypsum board, a plain background for the owners' diverse artifacts.

Kitchen has two windows just big enough to oversee driveway, frame views.

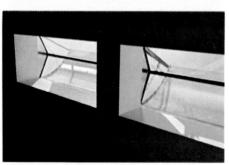

Living with nature affects the family in small ways. Water drums in a bedroom are bright red objects on which to store toys, left. Skylights, above, must be opened and closed and, seasonally, their roof reflectors adjusted manually —up in cold weather, down in summer to control heat gain. Because the sun also helps heat water for domestic uses, baths and showers are scheduled late in the day when the water has absorbed as much solar heat as it can and the house is at its warmest.

Two water preheaters—one under the laundry skylight, above, the other under the master bath skylight—help step up the temperature of ground water for hot water needs. Water goes first to the preheaters to be warmed by the sun, then to a conventional hot water heater. If the sun kicks the water up to, say, 120 degrees, and the heater is set for 130 degrees, only a comparatively little electricity is needed to complete the job.

Passive solar systems

Inexpensive to build, inexpensive to heat

This house is designed to get heating help from the sun with a greenhouse that collects heat, then radiates it upward via three-story-high vaults.

Living room glass doors gather sunlight. Wall above entrance door is squared off.

Solar collector panels were beyond the budget on this house, but solar energy is used nevertheless. Architect-owner Jefferson B. Riley achieved this in his AIA award-winning design by orienting the large gable end of the house toward the sunny south side, opening it up with glass, and keeping the building 16 feet deep so the sun's rays can reach everywhere. On this south side, a greenhouse, opposite, functions as a passive collector, whose warmth, through three-story-high solar vaults (see plans and sections, right) reaches the topmost story. The second and third floors, where the bedrooms are located, were set back from this sun-collecting gable end wall and given double-hung windows facing onto the sun-filled interior vaults. Interior windows in these rooms can open to share the warmth (and incidentally act as a family intercom system). Added heat comes from two wood stoves on the vault floors. And behind these more natural systems stands a forced-warm-air unit that uses oil fuel. To prevent leakage of heat, the connections to the greenhouse can be shut at night, and the large exterior windows are equipped with internal thermal shutters. Only four small windows pierce the north wall, where winter winds blow most strongly, and where neighbors are near.

The house stands on the border of a magnificent state forest in Connecticut. The parcel of wooded land had a grandeur that Barbara and Jefferson Riley could not pass up, so they planned a house that would live up to the costly site, but would be economical to build. To keep construction costs down, the house is small. Its ground floor extends 1½ inches beyond the 16-by-40-foot foundation. This avoids waste from 16-foot joists, and also allows for the 1½-inch Styrofoam insulation outside the foundation walls, enabling them to be used to store solar heat. Excess solar heat collected in the greenhouse circulates along these insulated foundation walls and is stored in the mass of the concrete for radiation at night. Exterior walls were constructed with 2-by-6-inch framing, instead of the usual 2-by-4, permitting thicker insulation to be used. *[Continued]*

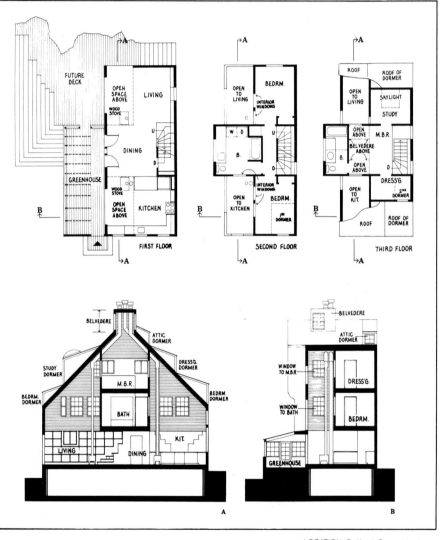

LOCATION: Guilford, Connecticut
SIZE: 1,200 square feet
ARCHITECT: Jefferson B. Riley of Moore Grover Harper PC

Plans and section, above: The first floor consists of the greenhouse (eventually opening to a large deck) and a large, interflowing public space. The second floor has two bedrooms and a bath, but a smaller square footage than the first because of the solar vaults that rise on either end of the south side. Interior windows bring vaults' warm air to bedrooms. Third floor is limited to a comfortable master suite, crowned by the belvedere.

Opposite: This is the south, energy-gathering façade. The greenhouse (whose windows are in graduated sizes for visual animation) acts as a passive solar collector and entrance, as well as plant room. Large second-floor windows bring more of the sun's heat to the pair of solar vaults on this side. From here, excluding the greenhouse, the building is only 16 feet deep, making it easy for the sun to penetrate.

The pleasing, somewhat nostalgic impact of the Jefferson Riley house, with its long gable, traditional double-hung windows, red-stained and natural clapboards, dormers, fanlight, and its intimate, personal spaces within, results from a great many allusions to the colonial homes and cottages indigenous to the locality. Yet the elements do not in any way combine to produce an imitation of any early form. Instead, it is clearly the house of a contemporary architect, made for a contemporary family that wanted to experience sun and air and forest views, and also sought a link to the enduring qualities of their historic area. The design by Mr. Riley, a partner in the architectural firm Moore Grover Harper in Essex, Connecticut, earned him an award of merit in the 1977 AIA Homes for Better Living Program.

Greenhouse is warmly welcoming.

Doors separate living area, entry.

Red, white, and wood combine for a bright kitchen, below, and open storage makes its visual contribution while saving money on cabinet work. Part of the kitchen reaches up three stories; part, under a bedroom, is one story high. Note unusual cabinets.

ROBERT PERRON

Although windows play a serious role in this energy-efficient house, the architect also used them for visual liveliness, as on the kitchen's front wall, above, where they step up in height. In less imaginative hands, they probably would have been of a size. The large vertical pipe is the furnace flue. Next to it, the wood stove flue rises. All heat pipes meet in the belvedere atop the house, radiating warmth as they go.

The stair hall is lined with bookshelves, far left; the rising flue is from a second wood stove near the living room. Near left: A view of the kitchen, taken from the interior window of the second-story bathroom (see plans on previous page), shows parts of two interior bedroom windows. The high spaces of the vaults are sided in beaded fir boards.

Passive solar systems

Trombe wall is low-tech collector

A massive south-facing concrete wall, sheathed by a double thickness of glass, is the basis of a solar system in the northeast.

The solar system of this house, designed by architect Douglas Kelbaugh for his own family, is an adaptation of the Trombe wall developed by Professor Felix Trombe in France. The architect says he "fell in love with the Trombe wall in 1973 after reading about it in the English architectural magazine *A.D.*" The Kelbaughs had been living in an 18th-century New Jersey farmhouse that had 2-foot-thick walls and they had grown fond of their "thermal and architectural presence." The Trombe wall in the Kelbaugh design is a 600-square-foot poured concrete wall, set 6 inches back from a continuous grid of glass that covers the southern face of the house. The wall absorbs and stores heat from the sun and radiates it into the house.

The climate and the site presented challenges: Princeton, New Jersey, has only a 50 to 55 percent sunshine factor during the winter and the only property they could find was close to neighboring houses that would cast shadows. By obtaining a zoning variance, Mr. Kelbaugh was able to push the house to the northern boundary of the 60-by-100-foot lot to clear the shadows and to save a large existing tree. This also gave the Kelbaughs a large single outdoor space, rather than the four relatively useless yards that the zoning code permitted. "As far as I know, this is the first Trombe wall built in this country," says the architect. "The advantages of this wall are many: its long life, architectural integration into the house, the mechanical simplicity." Insulation is important to the working of the Kelbaughs' passive solar system: 4 inches for walls, 9½ inches in the roof, 1 inch of polystyrene on the perimeter wall of the foundation. A fireplace is used in the winter for aesthetics and localized comfort. Auxiliary infrared heaters in the bath are seldom needed. There is a backup gas-fired hot air furnace. If he were to do it over, Mr. Kelbaugh says he would first provide a direct fresh air vent to the fireplace for combustion; second, enlarge the eave vents and/or install operable windows in the south wall to increase cross ventilation. By placing windows within the collector/storage wall, the architect did overcome one disadvantage of the Trombe wall, where storage elements usually take up the sunny side of the building where windows might be.

Concrete wall spans south façade; collects, stores, radiates heat from the sun.

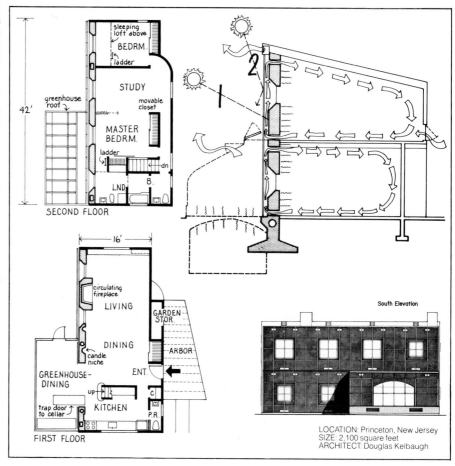

SECOND FLOOR

FIRST FLOOR

South Elevation

LOCATION: Princeton, New Jersey
SIZE: 2,100 square feet
ARCHITECT: Douglas Kelbaugh

Solar south wall, opposite, has a curtain of glass to trap heat absorbed by concrete Trombe wall. Plan, above, shows how windows are set into this wall to bring in natural light. A standard Lord and Burnham greenhouse leans against and works sympathetically with the Trombe wall.

Diagram, above, shows how winter sun (1) penetrates glass at nearly perpendicular angle, is trapped and heats wall. Chimney effect pulls cool air into wall's open core at the bottom and pours warm air out into rooms. In summer (2), rays hit wall at oblique angle and are reflected. Summer heat buildup is vented at eave.

Passive solar systems

Glass and masonry act as collector

Built on an Ozark mountain slope, this passive house collects and stores thermal energy in a south-facing wall.

A towering wall of glass, backed by 12-inch-thick masonry walls to store thermal energy collected through the south-facing glazed area, is the key element of this passive solar house designed by architect James Lambeth. The three-bedroom, two-bath house was built in the forested hills near Fayetteville, Arkansas, for a high school teacher and his wife, John and Mitzi Delaps, who requested a low-cost, high-energy-efficient house. They got that, plus much more. The building not only works with its environment, but the architect's integrative design skills made for a structure as handsome as it is energy efficient. The house is full of light and space; rising three stories high, it has adjacent outdoor living decks on each level. North and south openings provide natural ventilation, and air conditioning is required only two months of each year.

The south-facing glass wall, opposite, forms an 860-square-foot passive collector that supplies the house with 60 to 75 percent of all its heating needs. Reflective extensions (see drawing) of the east and west walls, designed to radiate heat back to this collector wall or to be shut during winter sunless days to provide additional insulation have yet to be added. The heat of the sun is stored in the 12-inch-thick masonry walls, built just inside the window wall. More thermal energy is stored in a stone-filled chamber located in the below-ground crawl space. When needed, this heat is distributed throughout the house by a duct system. An auxiliary electric heat pump provides heat when temperatures of the air in the rock-bed storage area are inadequate for heating.

Cost of the added materials for the solar system was $1,400, with a payback estimated in 9.33 years at today's energy costs. The solar system cost 1/40th the total project; standard flat-plate collectors typically cost 1/7th the total project, according to the AIA *Energy Notebook*. For this reason, cost cannot be used as an argument against passive solar architecture, James Lambeth points out, as many decisions require no dollar outlay at all. The owners' anticipate average monthly energy bills of $30. Average energy costs for a comparable building would be $90 for an electric home; and $70 for a gas-operated home.

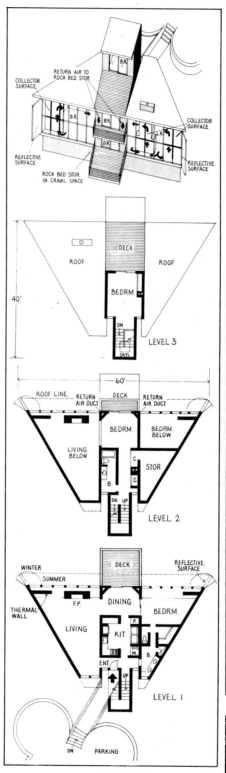

LOCATION: Fayetteville, Arkansas
SIZE: 2,000 square feet
ARCHITECT: James Lambeth

Orientation and insulation are also key factors in the design, resulting in the fan-shaped plan, above, with the north wall as the shortest end. Cold northerly winds are deflected to the windowless sides of the house.
Drawings of the Delap house show how the southern elevation is open to winter sun and protected from summer sun by a 4-foot overhang. At the same time, the canted east and west walls open the house's interior to both sun and views of the Ozark Hills.

NORMAN McGRATH

The whimsical Mickey Mouse driveway, left, was designed in honor of Mitzi and John Delaps' son, Dax, born just as the house was completed. John and Mitzi Delaps relax in their light-filled, high-reaching living room, right, where a masonry fireplace also acts as a thermal mass for energy collected through the south-facing wall of glass. It and masonry walls on each side are painted black on the exterior to better absorb the sun's rays.

Passive solar systems

Small, ingenious, and energy-wise

Instead of a central heating system, this house — built with rustic and recycled elements — uses a massive heating-cooking stove for its main source of heat.

The owners of a parcel of Massachusetts oceanside land, Mr. and Mrs. Richard Gummere, Jr., wanted a simple, low-budget design that would keep them as independent of high-cost fuels as possible. Their architect, Alex Wade, designed an energy-wise house that is oriented to the south and east for sun and views. To keep costs down, and to overcome an unusual number of difficulties (recounted in his own book, *30 Energy-Efficient Houses ... You Can Build),* he helped build the house of recycled and salvaged fixtures and parts. In his book he tells how the large areas of south-facing glass were designed to absorb heat. Thermal barriers are badly needed over the doors and windows, however, and so "the south-facing glass absorbs lots of heat in the daytime, but loses it again at night." The compact house — a little over 600 square feet in all — has a mix of heating systems that offers choices to fit fuel prices, temperatures, moods. Instead of spending money on a central heating system, a massive Glenwood heating/cooking stove was installed at the center of the open two-level design. It can burn coal, wood, or gas. The stove has a gas cooking surface and a coal section for general heating. It is backed up by a small, automatic, gas-fired circulating heater for periods when the house is unoccupied or the weather is particularly severe. There are also auxiliary stoves that burn wood; the bath and study, which can be closed off, have electric baseboards.

For snugness, insulation went on the outside of the house, then rough pine siding. Smooth 3-inch-thick fir planking forms the interior walls, the wood beautifully mellowed by sea breezes that swept through the house before it was completed. The house is essentially one large lofty space, with small sleeping areas opening off it. It is supported by 6-by-6-inch posts spaced 10 feet apart. The exposed post and beam construction allows the use of high areas: Bunks are tucked under the roof; balconies, skylights, and the tall space make the small plan seem spacious. "The wonderful vertical feeling lifts your spirit as you come in the doors," says Mrs. Gummere.

In the open two-story living area, stoves back up to exposed central chimney.

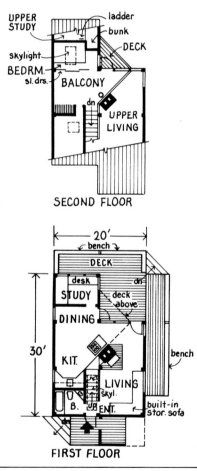

LOCATION: Duxbury, Massachusetts
SIZE: 600 square feet
ARCHITECT: Alex Wade

A painted terne roof, made by the architect, is as dramatic as a red signal flag in contrast to the mellowed rough pine structure, opposite. Plans, above, show the ingenious use of space on all levels. An extra wood stove, right center, is located on an upstairs balcony between two sleeping spaces. A skylight and recycled windows brighten the entry, right. Stairway just inside was salvaged from an old house.

28

Drive leads to entry on north.

Levels of house overlook potato fields.

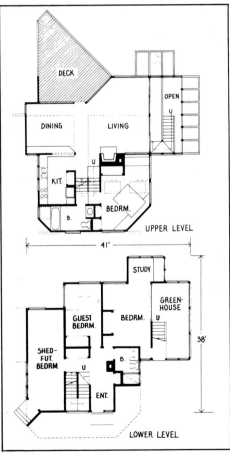

DECK

OPEN

DINING   LIVING

U

KIT.

U

B.   BEDRM.

UPPER LEVEL

41'

STUDY

GREEN-HOUSE

GUEST BEDRM.   BEDRM.

U

SHED-FUT. BEDRM.

U

B.

38'

ENT.

LOWER LEVEL

LOCATION: Watermill, New York
SIZE: 2,000 square feet
ARCHITECT: Alfredo De Vido

The site itself was admirably suited to solar energy: Its open side and slant are to the sun-snatching south, and the south and east also offer the best views of the endless potato fields. On the less sunny north, top, are the approach, tall trees, and few windows.

Passive solar systems
Greenhouse maximizes solar benefits

While plants and people bask in sunlight, the glazing on this house captures and traps the sun's radiant energy.

A striking greenhouse, the handsome focal point of this cedar-clad vacation house, built on the edge of a Southampton, New York, potato field, not only provides a sun-filled space for plants and people but captures and traps solar heat for adjacent rooms. In the multilevel design by architect Alfredo De Vido, the south-facing greenhouse stretches up from the ground to the mid-level living room. There the two areas are joined by sliding glass doors, and these are opened whenever solar heat is wanted in the social spaces. The house has such a wonderful rapport with nature, say the owners, that solar energy per se is never on their minds: They do not have to stop every few minutes to consider how hot or cold a room is or to open or close windows and doors. Much of this ease has to do with the interflow of greenhouse and rooms, rooms and decks (see plan), and the placement of glass on every side and in roofs, too. What the owners are happily aware of is the beauty of the house, its extraordinary views in and from every room, its exhilarating high spaces and great beams of natural light, as well as its comfortable temperatures.

To control those temperatures after sundown in cool weather, or on cloudy days, the glass doors between the living spaces and the greenhouse are kept closed to confine heat in the living area. A conventional heating system with an oil furnace also serves this part of the house. For the lower part, instead of going to a two-zone oil heating system, the architect decided on supplementary electric heat to save costs. In the owners' first year in the house, with a winter of extra-cold weather, auxiliary heat was rarely needed. In summer, no air conditioning was necessary: Good cross ventilation invites breezes; and the house has several strategically located skylights that can be opened so rising hot air is whisked out. On hot days, doors between the living room and greenhouse are closed to keep excess heat out of the living areas. In the upper part of the greenhouse, a ventilation fan controlled by a thermostat goes on when the temperature is too high, so plants will not burn. The glass-roofed study facing east, on the lower level, is a miniature echo of the handsome two-level greenhouse it abuts.   [*Continued*]

For the study: natural light and views.

A balcony sits high in the greenhouse.

Deep tub in a woodsy, skylighted bath.

Adjoining bedroom is on upper level.

To begin with, the co-owners of this house never had solar heating in mind when they met with their architect. What they did have in mind was a greenhouse. They had decided it would make a wonderful focal point for the vacation house they wanted to build, especially since one of the owners, Lynn Whitton, wanted plenty of indoor garden space: Her love of house plants had led her to a part-time business venture — a plant-decorating service. Architect De Vido put one and one together — greenhouse and solar energy — and the two women enthusiastically accepted the idea of having the sun help with the heating as well as with plant life. What Mr. De Vido had in mind for his passive solar design was what is known as "the greenhouse effect." This physical phenomenon involves radiation and the transmitting properties of glass. Shortwave radiation from the sun can pass through glass. When the sunlight strikes nonreflective surfaces, it is absorbed and radiated back as heat. This radiation is of a longer wavelength that cannot quickly escape through glass. It is this trapped solar heat in the greenhouse part of the De Vido design that is used to help warm the house.

Every room in the greenhouse/dwelling offers exciting angles, streams of light, close and faraway scenes. For example, someone sitting downstairs on the living room sofa can glance up, through both a high glass wall in the top-level bedroom and a skylight nearby, to see a nicely framed piece of sky. Also, beyond doors from living room to greenhouse is a 3-foot-wide viewing ledge. "In winter, looking over the plants, seeing snow beyond, and feeling so warm from the sun has the effect of being in Switzerland and seeing those bright ski slopes where skiers are comfortable without heavy jackets," says one owner. The open-plan social areas are also linked to a deck that has its longest side angled to face farm scenery on the east. Upper deck is more secluded and has a "view of forever."

Dining, living, and kitchen areas, opposite, are largely defined by changes in ceiling heights. These are flat only below the upper deck; otherwise they are soaring, sharply angled. Owners say the open space is fabulous for entertaining.

Throughout the house, opposite and above, a symphony of naturals comes from the wood of floor planks and ceilings, from tree trunks seen through windows, farm and woodlands outside and plants within, each one carefully installed. Enjoyment of indoor gardening led to Lynn Whitton's Thumbs Up Green plant service, which involves decorating with plants.

The study, a mini-greenhouse, is, with its built-in desk, top left, a "magnificent place to work," says one of the owners, an advertising consultant. "I can look up at night and see millions of stars and look down and see the greenhouse." Greenhouse balcony, top right, has stairs to plant area below.

A bathroom at the top of the house, middle left, has an in-the-woods look, a luxuriously deep tub. Over the banquette in the bedroom, middle right, is glass lookout to the living room and greenhouse. For the kitchen, left, and elsewhere, low-maintenance materials include easy-care wood, aluminum thermal break windows and doors, plain painted walls, and Formica laminate countertops.

Ninety metal drums collect and store heat

Stacks of 55-gallon metal drums, filled with water, form the south wall of this solar house. Huge insulated doors keep heat in.

This remarkable house, made up of 11 metal zomes clustered together and offering 2,000 square feet of space, is 85 percent heated by the sun. Designed by its owner, Steve Baer, a talented designer, inventor, and mathematician, the house is heated by one of his inventions — the drumwall. Ninety 55-gallon metal drums, filled with water, are stacked up to form walls on the four south-side zomes of the house. The drums are painted black on their sunlight-catching side and placed behind glass, which helps retain the solar heat they collect. Huge insulated doors, operated on winches, open and close over the drumwalls like a country mailbox. On sunny winter days they are open to trap heat and warm the water in the drums. At night they are closed when the air turns cold, but heat continues to radiate from the drums to warm the rooms. In summer the doors are closed during the day and opened at night when the temperature drops. This keeps the water cool so when the house tends to warm up the next day, the water absorbs the heat like a natural air conditioner. To prevent rusting, a corrosion-preventing mixture is added to the water.

Insulated doors: Open they expose drumwalls to solar heat; closed they trap heat gained from the sun.

Steve Baer began the experiment that led to the zome form for his house by reshaping abandoned car roofs that he bought for a quarter apiece. A thousand car roofs later the basic layout and shape of his house had evolved. Mr. Baer found the zomes (a zome is a geometric shape with a parallel zone in it) worked better for housing than domes. "It's a more flexible shape. A zome can be stretched out, joined together with other zomes, and makes very satisfying free-form building." The house is built on a concrete slab with a wooden sill. The walls are insulated aluminum panels, similar to those used in trailers and airplanes. These walls were laminated locally and then put up by the Baers and a group of friends, none of whom had had professional construction training. The aluminum panels are pop-riveted together with aluminum strips, at the joints, and the seams are protected with a silicone sealant. This kind of construction allows the metal outer "skin" to contract and expand as the temperature changes. [Continued]

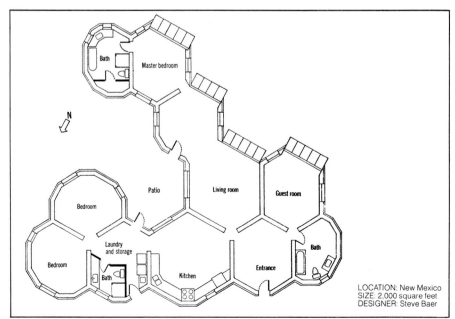

LOCATION: New Mexico
SIZE: 2,000 square feet
DESIGNER: Steve Baer

ROBERT LAUTMAN

A cluster of aluminum zomes, above, form this unique solar-heated house near Albuquerque, New Mexico. Louvered Skylids gather heat on the roofs, ventilator fans draw in the breezes, fireplaces on the north side provide supplemental heat.

Drumwalls, right, form the simple collector system. Opened to the sun's rays, they collect and store heat to be radiated into the rooms of the house at night when huge insulated doors, operated on winches, are swung closed to keep the heat inside.

Steve Baer's eleven-zome plan, left, forms a V with the living room and kitchen at the center, and the children's wing and master suite at either end of the honeycomb design.

Skylids bring sun to areas not directly heated by drumwalls. **Windmill pumps water from well; it runs to house by gravity.**

Automatic louvers under each Skylid control the sun's rays. **Baer kitchen illustrates marvelous interior space of a zome.**

ROBERT LAUTMAN

Overhead Skylids are another of Steve Baer's devices for warming his house with solar energy. The Skylids are inserted in some of those rooms not directly heated by drumwalls: the kitchen, the foyer, and one of the children's rooms. An aluminum automatic louver under each skylight controls the sunlight. "Again a perfectly simple idea. The Skylid has no switches or wire or motors to go haywire," Steve Baer says. Two Freon gas-filled canisters on each side of one panel respond to the changing temperature and cause the louvers to move. When the sun spills into the room it is retained by the floor, a concrete slab painted with red driveway paint, and by the adobe-faced walls. These elements slowly release the heat during cooler parts of the day and at night. To take advantage of the desert breezes each zome has a ventilator with a fan to bring the fresh air inside. Electricity from the local power plant operates the lighting, refrigerator, and laundry equipment. Propane gas is used for cooking; the water source is a well. A windmill pumps the water up and it runs into the house by gravity. Steve Baer designed solar collectors to heat the water supply. Each solar collector is a rectangular flat-plate collector angled to catch the sun's rays, and its angle is adjusted from season to season. The collectors are connected to a water storage tank in the master bedroom bathroom and to another near the kitchen that supplies this room, the laundry room, and children's bath with an additional hot water supply.

In the living room, opposite, adobe walls, red-painted concrete floors, drumwalls, are equally pleasant interior elements; overhead a stained-glass skylight by Carol Caroling transforms sunshine into jewellike colors.

Skylids control warm rays of the sun

On a southern California ranch, a house made up of a cluster of zomes is warmed by the sun through nine louvered skylights.

This house is on a working ranch north of Santa Barbara, but it is like no other ranch house ever seen. It consists of a U-shaped cluster of zomes, topped by Skylids that let the heat of the sun into the house to make it almost totally independent of any fossil fuels. It was built for Jake and Nancy Kittle, both conservationists, who wanted a solar-heated house on their ranch in California. Interested in a passive solar system for collecting and storing the sun's heat, they found what they wanted when they saw the solar house (preceding pages) designed and owned by Steve Baer, of Zomeworks. Charting daily temperatures at the ranch, Steve Baer worked with architect Dick Henry, who designed a nine-zome house that could be heated by using twelve south-facing skylights as collectors. Freestanding concrete block walls and tile floors within the zomes, well insulated on the outside, absorb and store the heat of the sun, and release it slowly at night. To control sunlight in summer and prevent loss of heat at night, insulated shutters, a Baer invention called Skylids, are housed beneath each skylight. Freon gas, moving back and forth between two canisters according to the heat of the sun, or lack of it, open the shutters during sunny weather and close them during very cloudy periods and at night. A manual override allows the owner to close the shutters entirely in summer. Although the skylights do not collect all the heat required, even on an overcast day there can be a good deal of heat gain. For supplementary heat, stoves in the kitchen and master bedroom and masonry fireplaces in the living room and office burn wood. The kitchen range uses propane gas, and electricity is only used for lighting and appliances. Water for the house is heated in two flat-plate collectors mounted on the roof of the master bedroom wing. It is stored in a triple-insulated water heater. The exterior of the house is redwood shiplap sheathing, to which a bleaching oil was applied. The shingles on the roof are composition for reasons of scale, fire protection, and economy.

Interior concrete walls and a terra-cotta floor laid in cement form the storage part of the passive system. [*Continued*]

GLEN ALLISON

At the top of a knoll set with ancient oaks, the house, above, is made up of nine zomes, sheathed on the exterior with beautiful redwood shiplap siding, recycled from California wine vats.

The zomes, strung together in a casual-seeming U, form a loop around a south-facing patio, right. Entry to the house can be through this patio (see plan on the following pages) or through a protected doorway on the north.

The sun's radiant energy is channeled through Skylids installed in the top of the zomes, left. Zomeworks, inventor and manufacturer of the Skylids, advises installing them on an east-west axis. Heat of the sun automatically opens and closes the Skylid shutters.

Freestanding walls of concrete blocks, their hollows filled with extra concrete to make them more efficient, were built just inside the walls of the zomes. In order to store heat a masonry wall must be insulated; in this house the layered walls of the zomes do the job. Zome frameworks were prefabricated in the Zomeworks shop in Albuquerque, brought by truck to California, and erected quickly on the site. A plywood skin was attached to the outside of the frame, and windows were cut in. Between the plywood and the outside sheathing of salvaged redwood a layer of 15-pound felt was sandwiched. On the inside of the prefabricated frames 4 inches of Fiberglas-insulating batting is covered with gypsum wallboard.

GLEN ALLISON

The living room of the house includes two zomes, above, with a built-in sofa that is especially high to accommodate the 6-foot-plus original owners. Stained-glass windows around the door, above left, are an example of the craftsmanship that abounds in the house. It includes the efforts of a dozen craftsmen and a lifetime collection of southwestern arts and crafts.

Kitchen/dining room is in one zome, right and left. The old range in the photo at left uses bottled gas; a porcelain stove, in the photo right, has been converted to burn wood, which is plentiful on the ranch. Kitchen cabinetry has been fitted to the geometry of the zomes. The counters and island are 42 inches high, again to accommodate the height of the owners.

LOCATION: Santa Barbara vicinity, California
SIZE: 2,100 square feet
ARCHITECT: Dick Henry
SOLAR CONSULTANT: Steve Baer

0 5 10   25 FT.

MASTER
BEDRM.

B

LIVING

GUEST

STO.

KITCHEN

B

ENTRY

OFFICE

Floor plan, left, reveals that no two zomes in the house are exactly alike in size or shape. The floor area totals 2,100 square feet; the height of the zomes adds to the spacious quality of the design of the house.

A solar house built by its owners

Plans can be ordered for this house, built for under $10,000, with a do-it-yourself solar system that stores a day's heat for nighttime use.

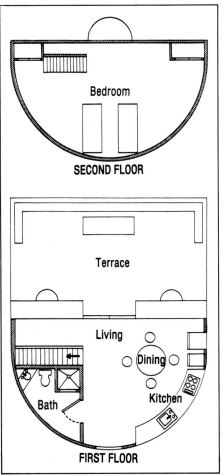

SECOND FLOOR

Bedroom

FIRST FLOOR

Terrace

Living

Dining

Kitchen

Bath

LOCATION: Southern Illinois
SIZE: 650 square feet
DESIGNER: Michael E. Jantzen

The Jantzens' solar system is seen at a glance: sunlight shines through plastic bubble windows and fiberglass roof sections, opposite, directly into heat storage tanks filled with water that absorbs the day's heat and stores it for nighttime use. Plans, above, show the design simplicity of the house; living area below, bedroom above.

This futuristic-looking solar-heated house was designed and built by Mike and Ellen Jantzen in Illinois using local materials, unskilled labor, and the simplest technology. Among its parts: the prefabricated dome of a silo, plexiglass skylight bubbles, cables, and boat winches. The passive solar system consists of the skylights used as windows with transparent roof panels over them and water storage tanks under them that absorb the sun's heat during the day and give it off at night—plus thorough insulation. Notched Mylar-clad panels reflect extra sunshine through the transparent roof panels below it into storage tanks that also serve as window seats inside the house. At sundown the tanks are closed, to be opened later when the house needs heat; the closed lids form window banquettes. Open, water tanks radiate stored-up heat. On hot days, the roof panel is closed to shade windows, reflect heat away from the house. The panels are controlled by cables and boat winches. Plexiglas skylight bubbles were used as windows because they catch sun from greater angles than do normal windows. Steel tubes conduct heat through the water and antifreeze solution that fills the two 16-cubic-foot insulated steel tanks.

Though neither architect nor engineer, Mike Jantzen wanted to see if he could design and build. He succeeded, keeping the cost of the house under $10,000, including furniture and appliances. Because the Jantzens wanted a vacation house to use mostly on weekends, they did not need to build a solar system that would store heat for more than one night and the house could be minimal in its design. Mr. Jantzen worked without blueprints, designing and building the house like sculpture. The exterior is plywood, corrugated steel, and half a prefabricated silo top. Prefabricated wood arches made for farm machine sheds are the vertical and horizontal structural supports. The house is well insulated; one portable electric heater can warm the whole building on a cloudy day. Even so, Mike Jantzen advises anyone building the house, for which plans are available, to use even more insulation. [*Continued*]

On hot summer days, closed roof panels shade windows.

Sun shines through windows and fiberglass roof sections.

The most important single factor in the heating and cooling of the Jantzen house is to be found in the efficiency of the insulation. "Insulate as much as you can," Mike Jantzen advises. "Also use plastic film as a vapor barrier whenever you can. This will help cut down on the general air flow through the walls." Fiberglass insulation was used on the lower level of the Jantzen house, polyurethane foam was sprayed on the bedroom walls, protected from flammability by ½-inch plaster. Wiring is in the floor, well away from the polyurethane. "Be sure to know your local codes concerning the use of polyurethane foams," Mr. Jantzen warns. "The material is flammable and must be coated with a fireproof substance."

The Jantzens have also built a solar greenhouse and a solar sauna on their Illinois vacation property. In the greenhouse the sun enters through a wall of clear curved plexiglass, heats up a wall of rocks. A sliding, insulated, corrugated fiberglass cover keeps heat from escaping at night. In the summer the cover is left off at night to let heat escape. The floor is Styrofoam covered with pebbles to hold moisture. An underground duct circulates warm air to keep greenhouse plants comfortable on long winter nights. Water is turned on for five minutes on a sunny day to allow humidity to rise. Temperatures reach 120 degrees. Plans for all three of the solar structures can be ordered from Michael Jantzen, Box 173, Carlyle, Illinois 62231. House plans are $25; greenhouse plans, $20; and the sauna plan, $15.

Open water tank radiates stored-up heat.

North side of greenhouse has shaded shelves for pots.

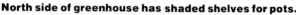

South side of greenhouse is a curve of clear plexiglass.

Particle-board cabinets hug curved kitchen wall.

Open trap door in bedroom admits warm air from downstairs.

Sauna is a 5-foot column of plexiglass with a skylight roof.

Ventilation system helps protect greenhouse from boilovers.

Sliding insulated cover keeps heat from escaping at night.

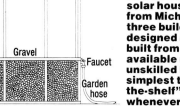

Heat vent
Exterior vent
Blower
Shelves
Air duct
Rock wall
Insulated air duct

Adjustable nozzle

Gravel

Faucet

Garden hose

Plans for the solar sauna, left, the greenhouse, above, as well as the do-it-yourself solar house, can be ordered from Michael Jantzen. All three buildings were designed by Mr. Jantzen to be built from inexpensive, available materials by unskilled labor, utilizing the simplest technology and "off-the-shelf" hardware whenever possible.

TOM YEE

45

The fiberfill quilting at the windows of the living room, far left, and master bedroom, left, is "the single best thing we discovered for a new or old house," says Roc Caivano. It cut fuel needs of the wood stove, opposite, in half.

About life in an energy-wise house: "We were surprised at how enjoyable it is to live this way. One gets a keener sense of the weather and it's a bit like sailing a boat—opening or closing soft, quilted curtains in response to the color of the morning sky or the number of stars you saw the night before is addictive."

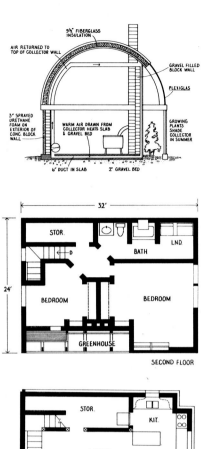

9½" FIBERGLASS INSULATION

AIR RETURNED TO TOP OF COLLECTOR WALL

GRAVEL FILLED BLOCK WALL

PLEXIGLAS

3" SPRAYED URETHANE FOAM ON EXTERIOR OF CONC. BLOCK WALL

WARM AIR DRAWN FROM COLLECTOR HEATS SLAB & GRAVEL BED

GROWING PLANTS SHADE COLLECTOR IN SUMMER

6" DUCT IN SLAB   2' GRAVEL BED

32'

24'

STOR.

LND.

BATH

D

BEDROOM   BEDROOM

GREENHOUSE

SECOND FLOOR

STOR.

KIT.

LIVING

U

STOVE

DINING

WARM AIR SOLAR COLLECTOR

GREENHOUSE

FIRST FLOOR

LOCATION: Bar Harbor, Maine
SIZE: 1,368 square feet
ARCHITECT: Roc Caivano

Plan, above: Air-lock entry through south-facing greenhouse, open-plan downstairs with centrally located stove, and minimal glass on north contribute to success of heating system. Trapped greenhouse air, heated by sun, enters house through ducts in slab (drawing, top). Curved roof, heavily insulated, was made from 2-by-10s ripped into strips. These were glued one over another to form arch. Span makes rooms seem larger.

BERT PERRON

Whimsical in design, wise in energetics

Built largely by the owners, a masonry and glass design, plus a working wood stove, keeps a passive solar house warm in Maine for $130 a year.

Much masonry, notable for its high heat-holding capacity; special insulation; and south-facing glass and plastic to let in sun are the strategic building elements of this passive solar design in Maine. On the west, where rooms may be added, the wall is mostly cedar and glass. On the other three sides, concrete blocks were dry-stacked—with only a little mortar used every few courses for stability—and 3 inches of polyurethane foam insulation (R-21) were sprayed on the outside. Then Bloc bond, a stuccolike cement that contains fiberglass reinforcement, was troweled over it and finished with latex paint. Bloc bond was also applied inside. (Note: Polyurethane foam gives off deadly gas when it burns, so it must be sandwiched between fireproof materials.) On the south, for an effective thermal wall, the concrete blocks were filled with gravel for more mass, painted dark brown to absorb solar energy, and covered with a wall of plastic on the outside to act as a vertical Trombe solar collector. To trap even more warmed air, a Plexiglas wall was added 4 feet out from the south-facing masonry wall, creating a two-story-high curved greenhouse (see section). There, vines are being cultivated for shade in summer. For a hot air system, ducts are imbedded in the slab. When solar heat warms the greenhouse air to 80 degrees Fahrenheit, a fan draws it into the ducts and the living quarters. In the process, the floor becomes radiant-heated and also serves as thermal storage. Two electric heaters, thermostatically controlled, rarely go on.

What Roc and Helen Caivano required, for themselves and daughter Katie, was an affordable and expandable dwelling that could be heated with free solar energy and easily available wood. The couple built the basic structure one summer with the help of a few artisans and several students from College of the Atlantic, where Mr. Caivano teaches. When you can build a house for $30,000 and heat it with sun plus $130 worth of wood a year in the cold reaches of Bar Harbor, you can afford to include a bit of whimsy in the design, says the architect Roc Caivano.

A roof designed to catch the sun

In a living room that basks under a translucent roof of fiberglass, it's like being outdoors all day.

Walls are glass, roof is translucent.

With a completely translucent roof, the sun comes right into the main room of this suburban Boston house, filling it with an abundance of natural light and the warmth of solar energy. Leland Cott of Gelardin/ Bruner/Cott architects accomplished this feat with the domestication of a material usually found only in industrial or commercial applications: sandwich panels of light-transmitting (insulating) fiberglass. Air conditioning and the roof's built-in insulation keep the room cool in summer; winter heating is minimal, thanks to the sun's energy. Beneath the innovative roof, two walls (facing south and east) are completely made of double-glazed sliding glass doors (left open to the garden when the weather is right). On the north and west, two wings of the house form an L to enclose the translucent-roofed living room. This L-shaped portion of Cott's design is a square-edged box of conventional sturdy framing and a 4-ply built-up roof behind a shallow parapet. New fiberglass and stucco coating on these exterior walls helps insulate them. Almost entirely closed on its two short walls and modestly opened on its long walls, the "solid" box is in high contrast to the building's elegant 900-square-foot open living room, which rises along its ridge to a height of 22 feet where it meets the wood walls.

The house sits on land that dips slowly to a pond at the south; a private tennis court is located just east of the structure. Approached from the west, its public side is deliberately understated, concealing from view the sun-gathering living space at its heart. Although the stair to the second floor is the only other space with a translucent ceiling, the main room's feeling of brightness and openness is extended into subsidiary spaces by other means. Ceilings over all the rest of the lower floor, for example, are of parallel aluminum channels with a dramatic mirror finish. The sides of the living room that are sheltered by the two-story L of conventionally roofed spaces are open to hall and stairs, kitchen and dining areas. Bright, comfortable, and a welcome contrast to the owners' former dark dwelling, "the house works for the way we live." [Continued]

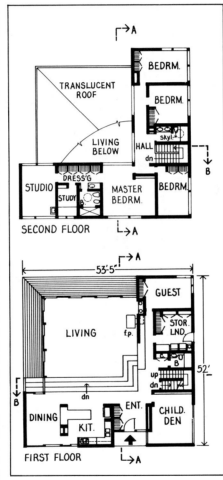

SECOND FLOOR

FIRST FLOOR

LOCATION: Suburban Boston, Massachusetts
SIZE: 5,571 square feet
ARCHITECT: Leland Cott of Gelardin/Bruner/Cott, Inc.

Plan of the house, above, shows how sky-roofed living room opens directly into dining area and kitchen. Upstairs bedroom hall overlooks the dramatic living room, as does the spacious master bedroom.

Two wings of the house form an L to enclose the translucent-roofed living room, opposite. New fiberglass and stucco coating on exterior walls helps insulate them.

Upstairs corridor overlooks skylit room.

Inside the translucent-roofed room it isn't really like being inside at all, so washed with sunlight is the space. The translucent panels are supported on aluminum beams, which also carry track lights for night lighting. Spectacular as the living room is, Cott's design is by no means a one-room house. Spaces open broadly into each other (see plan) — the entrance hall into the stairway, the kitchen into the dining area, and all of them into the living room. The single exceptions, downstairs, are a guest bedroom, a laundry/workroom, and a small study (used by the children for television watching), all of which have been given conventional privacy. Upstairs, the bedroom corridor is also open to the living room, and the master bedroom shares the room's space (but not its sounds) by overlooking it through a large triangular sheet of fixed glass. Next to the master bedroom are an office and studio for the parents.

MARIS/SEMEL

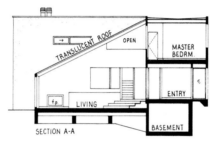

SECTION A-A

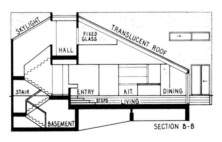

SECTION B-B

Inside the spectacular living room, opposite and above, the space is filled with sunlight that pours in overhead through the translucent panels supported on aluminum beams. These beams also carry track lights for night lighting. Flooring is 1-foot-square tiles of black slate; carpeted steps form extra seating for parties.

Ceilings over the rest of the lower floor, as in the dining room and kitchen, left, are of parallel aluminum channels with a dramatic mirror finish. The sparkle of sunlight is reflected in the mirror finish of these channels, as well as in the chrome and glass tables that furnish the spaces that open into one another.

Passive solar systems

Double walls, wind impellers, reduce chill

Minimal design saves energy in a tight, 1,400-square-foot house; but good planning makes every inch of the space work.

Minimal in size, modest in budget, this midwestern house has energy-saving techniques integrated into its design that keep monthly heating bills below $30. Built in 1975 at Rocky River, Ohio, for under $50,000 (probably $55,000 now, the architect-owner estimates), the energy-conservation features designed as an integral part of its structure then make it a cost-saving house today. Because the five-member Trout family likes to gather in one space, architect Will Trout designed a two-story living room at one end of the house—then devised some ingenious ways to keep chilly winter winds from sapping all the heat from the glass-enclosed room. Wood cross braces, made from massive 12-by-12-inch timbers, are set over the glass area. The cross braces are designed to set the wind in motion, circulating escaping warm indoor air over the glass. Recessed 6 inches into the heavy timbers, the insulated glass is also somewhat shielded from direct winds. Wind impellers like those over the living room's upper window areas also cover other second-story windows, and on the ground floor, panels slide over windows and doorways in severe weather.

Another method of saving house heat is the double construction of outside walls, designed to enclose a layer of heated air. Framed by standard 2-by-4-inch wood studs, the walls have an additional 2-by-2-inch framework. In the space between the double wall construction, heated indoor air circulates in a warming stream. The warm air is pulled into the air channel, on the windward side of the house, by wind currents at the base of the walls. A forced-air system heats and cools the house through ducts under it and upstairs. The wood first floor also gains radiant heat from warmth underneath it. Average heat bill: $28.50 monthly.

The façade of the center section of the essentially one-room-wide house stands taller than the flat roof over it to provide a screen for solar hot water panels that could be installed on this roof area should the Trouts decide to do so. A limited water supply, wrapped in heat tape and powered by an auxiliary generator, is now part of the house's backup systems.   [*Continued*]

Yellow and white graphic stripes add color to cedar-clad house.

Breezeway serves as sheltered entry   **Barn-door-like panels slide over window.**

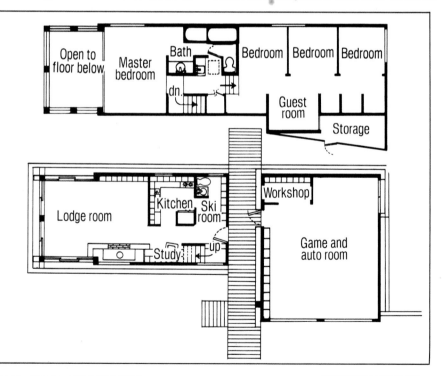

Plans, above, show the long, essentially one-room-deep scheme of the Trout house. Open breezeway connects house and garage under cover. On the second level, master bedroom overlooks the two-story-high living room; boys' bunkrooms are atop garage. The all-wood bath is multicompartmented, with sliding doors that divide parents' and children's sections for simultaneous use.

LOCATION: Rocky River, Ohio
SIZE: 1,400 square feet
ARCHITECT: Will Trout

Cross-brace framing of massive timbers serves as windbreak on the two-story-high living room that has glass walls on three sides. Sliding glass doors on the lower portion open the room to views of the river and to boats just outside.

The Trout house fits the family of five like a glove. It is flexible and informal to match their life-style precisely. Detailed with exceptional thoughtfulness — built-in furniture, storage for every need, low-maintenance materials — it is a house for ease and enjoyment, not one that rules and runs the family. "I wanted a house that I could be proud of," said Will Trout, "but one that was relaxing and not 'demanding' of me all the time." In planning it, activities and ways of living had first consideration. Because the family always seems to spend its time together, almost half the house was given over to one communal living space for relaxing, dining, working, studying, and cooking. The same viewpoint is seen upstairs, in the children's "bunkhouse" over the garage. Add-on board walls provide partial privacy in the sleeping rooms, with shared adjacent communal areas for watching TV, playing, family projects. Downstairs, the large garage serves as a generous storehouse for cars, bikes, and sports equipment; but cleared out it can be a spacious play and party space as well.

Open shelves divide dining area from kitchen; compact study area is under stairs.

TOM YEE

Master bedroom overlooks living room.

L-shaped kitchen has lots of storage.

Boys' dorm has changeable partitions.

Garage has compartmented storage.

Boats on the walls, bikes go overhead.

A much-used fireplace has a metal firebox and fireback reflector that can be a substitute heater for the house. Positioned to serve both sitting and dining areas in the two-story-high living space, the fireplace's exposed flue also radiates heat as it continues up through the master bedroom overhead.

Active solar systems

Unlike the passive solar designs we have just been looking at, active solar collectors appear to be relatively independent elements that can be organized and operated quite apart from the building — although you will see that the more the design of an energy-conscious house is integrated to work with the sun in all its aspects, the more energy-efficient the house will be. For that reason, many of the houses in the forty-six-page active solar section that follows this introduction will actually be hybrids — the term used to describe houses that combine active and passive elements in their solar design.

Using mechanical means — pumps, fans, automatic controls — active solar systems provide an energy system that works with less participation on the part of the occupants, not unlike the conventional heating we have all become accustomed to — once set, the thermostat essentially controls the mechanical system. The solar heat systems designed to replace, or in most cases supplement, these conventional heating systems consist of collectors to absorb the sun's radiation, ducts or pipes to transport the heat collected, and a means to store it.

The active solar houses we have included in the following pages use either simple solar collector devices made at the building site or factory-made products. In either case, the design considerations were the same: to provide a collector that could use the sun's rays to heat an absorber through which air or liquid is circulated to heat the house, either directly or via a heat storage unit. In all active solar collectors, air or liquid is heated as it passes over or through an absorber exposed to the sun. By far the most common collectors used by the houses in this book are in the shape of flat panels that have the appearance of a dark window or a skylight. Other collectors use curved shapes; some incorporate reflectors to focus or concentrate the sun's rays.

The relatively simple flat-plate collector has found the widest application in the new solar energy industry because of the low cost of its fabrication, installation, and maintenance as compared to higher temperature heat collection shapes. Also, flat-plate collectors can be easily incorporated into traditional or modern building design, as the houses that follow will show, provided the tilt and orientation are properly calculated. Flat-plate collectors utilize direct as well as diffuse solar radiation, and can attain 250 degrees Fahrenheit, which is well above the moderate temperatures needed for space heating, cooling, and domestic hot water.

Collectors of any kind need an uninterrupted southern exposure. They work best if they face the low winter sun directly — just a few degrees west of due south — and are tilted up at an angle that equals the latitude of the site plus 10 degrees. The microclimate is important in all of these calculations, it should be noted, and all systems must be designed to adjust to regional differences. Active energy systems are usually designed to provide up to 40 to 60 percent of the heat required. To accomplish this, the size of the collector area in square feet may range from 30 to 50 percent of the heated floor space. A 2,000-square-foot house would require a 600- to 1,000-square-foot collector.

Flat-plate Collectors

A flat-plate collector generally consists of an absorbing plate, often metallic (copper, aluminum, or steel), which may be flat, corrugated, or grooved; painted black to increase absorption of the sun's heat; insulated on its underside to minimize heat loss; and covered with a transparent (glass or plastic) cover sheet to trap heat within the collector and reduce convective cooling of the absorber. The captured solar heat is removed from the absorber by means of a transfer medium, generally air or treated water, which is heated as it passes through or near the absorbing plate. The heated transfer medium is transported to points of use or to storage depending on energy demand.

There are three types of flat-plate collectors used by the houses in this book. They include air-cooled collectors, water-cooled collectors, and open-water collectors.

The majority use water or antifreeze solution as the transport medium. The liquid — contained in pipes or channels — is heated as it passes through the absorber plate of the collector and then is pumped to a storage tank, transferring its heat to the storage medium. To prevent freezing, corrosion, or leaks in these liquid-cooled systems, which are efficient collectors and transporters of heat, oil or water treated with corrosion inhibitors is being used as the transport medium and/or the collectors are being designed to drain into storage during periods of noncollection.

Open-water collectors use corrugated metal panels painted black and covered with a transparent cover sheet. The panels provide open troughs in the corrugations for trickling water to be fed from a supply at the top of the roof to a collection gutter at the base, where it is then transported to storage.

In an air system, air circulating around the collector plate picks up heat and is moved either into the rooms or into a rock-filled storage bin. An air system has the advantage of relatively simple hardware and no potential of leaks, freezing, or corrosion; the disadvantage of air systems is the necessity for large ducts and storage (several tons of rock). Water systems require less than half the storage volume of an equivalent air system, and their thin pipes are less difficult to accommodate in the house.

Storage

Water has the highest heat capacity per pound of any ordinary material. It is also very inexpensive and so it has become an attractive storage and heat transfer medium. It does require a storage tank, which adds some cost. The storage tank is usually insulated to reduce conductive heat losses. Heat is generally transferred to and from storage by a working fluid circulated by an electric pump. The heated working fluid itself may be placed in storage or its heat transferred to the storage tank by a heat exchanger. The process of heat transfer to water is more efficient than to rock and therefore less surface for the heat exchanger is required. With water storage, proximity of storage to the collector is not as critical as with rock storage. Also, compared to rock storage, water occupies a comparatively small volume.

Rock storage, however, is the other common method of heat storage, most often associated with air-cooled flat-plate collectors. Pebble beds or rock piles contained in an insulated storage unit have sufficient heat capacity to provide heat for extended sunless periods. The rock storage is heated as air from the collector is forced through the rock container by a blower. Again, rock storage requires approximately 2½ times the volume of water storage, assuming the same temperature range — but, as some of the houses that follow will show, it can be used to advantage in some solar designs.

Vacuum-tube Collectors

One of the exceptions to the flat-plate collector dominance of our active solar house systems is the first house in the section, which uses a vacuum-tube collector. This collector consists of individual tube assemblies of tempered glass, reminiscent of fluorescent lights. Each collector-within-the collector consists of three glass tubes inserted one inside another: an outer tube, 2 inches in diameter; a black-coated intermediate tube, filled with water to be heated by the sun and returned to storage; and an inner tube that supplies fresh water from the storage tank. The outer tube serves as the cover enclosure and the space between it and the absorber tube is under vacuum pressure, which eliminates condensation and convection losses and explains the name — evacuated tube — often given to collectors such as these. Since the supply and return flow of the heat transfer medium are within each tube, they are simply connected at one end to horizontal manifolds with supply and return headers.

Because the round tubes receive radiation from all angles with less reflection loss and also utilize a wider range of diffuse radiation, the tubular collectors perform better than flat-plate designs on a day-long basis, especially during diffuse and cloudy sky conditions. It is a water-cooled system, and storage for the sun's heat is in an insulated storage tank like those used in other liquid systems.

Heating Systems

Active solar systems supply only a percentage of the space heating and domestic hot water needs of most designs, and so they must work with conventional heating, which is usually distributed either by forced-air systems (in which warm air is ducted from a furnace to separate outlets or registers in each room) or by hydronic systems (in which hot water is circulated from a boiler to baseboard hot water radiators). Solar systems usually are designed to work with forced-air systems, but with duct sizes that are larger than those used with conventional fuel heating in order to carry low-temperature air efficiently.

Some of the active solar systems work with a solar-assisted heat pump. Whereas solar collectors absorb and distribute "free" heat from the sun's radiation, heat pumps draw "free" heat out of winter's cold air. Simply put, a heat pump moves heat. It cools a house in the summer like an air conditioner by moving heat from the inside to the outside. In the winter, it heats the house by doing just the opposite — moving heat from outdoors to indoors, consid-

erably concentrated and enhanced. Because heat pumps work most efficiently when the air or water they extract heat from is about 50 degrees Fahrenheit, and because solar collectors are most efficient when the temperatures collected from them are low — less than 100 degrees Fahrenheit — solar energy and heat pumps have become allies.

Costs

The cost of an active solar system depends on the design and size of the house it will serve, climatic conditions where it is being built, and the type and size of the system chosen. In the 1976 HUD demonstration program, combined solar heating and hot water systems for single-family houses ranged in cost from $5,000 to $19,000. The cost for domestic hot water was only about $1,000 to $2,500. High first costs are a factor in adding an active solar system to a new house. But life-cycle costing — the idea that an appliance costs what you pay to buy it plus what it costs you to run it during its lifetime — must be considered in any buying decisions that involve the use of energy. Fossil fuels, the alternative to solar power, can only grow more expensive. As fuel prices go up, monetary savings from solar energy will be greater. As people become more aware of energy problems, the resale value of a house that saves on heating bills will increase. Tax incentives for solar heating installation also help reduce high first costs. And the earlier anyone joins the growing energy-conservation forces in this country, the less the world's energy resources are going to be used up.

Nevertheless, active solar systems rank as a major financial decision — and require all the care that such decisions always involve. First cost must be weighed against collector efficiency when comparing collectors. A relatively inexpensive collector with a low efficiency may be a poor choice when compared to a more expensive one that captures and delivers the sun's energy more efficiently. All other things being equal, the National Solar Heating and Cooling Information Center advises that "the collector that delivers more heat per dollar should be selected."

The center also stresses the importance of warranties, and for its fourth demonstration cycle, HUD will require a one-year warranty by the installer, providing parts and labor to repair or replace a defective installation, backed up by a five-year warranty by the collector manufacturer on the collector itself.

Inventing the Future

Liquid and air active systems — in their various guises — can be seen in place on the active solar houses that follow. They will demonstrate, like the passive houses before them, how far we have come in harnessing the abundant energy of the sun. It's important to note that the owners of these systems decided to look to the sun for energy before adequate standards and warranties could be worked out. Their experiences, some costly, some merely annoying, become part of the growing wealth of solar knowledge we can all now share. If, as some fuel company ads have suggested, solar technology is a 21st-century phenomenon, the architects, engineers, and homeowners whose combined foresight and willingness to experiment brought these houses into being must be counted among those who are aware "that we can make our life today the shape of tomorrow's future."

Built on Long Island marshland, the house had to be constructed on wood piles with living areas elevated on the second floor, the mechanical areas and a carport below (see section above). The solar collectors face due south at an angle of 57½ degrees from the horizontal. Given this angle, the entire house, above and left, was designed on a strong diagonal; the architect working with cardboard models as he sculpted the exciting shapes to come.

Glass tubes capture the sun's rays.

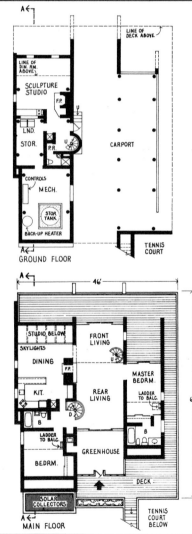

GROUND FLOOR

MAIN FLOOR

LOCATION: Quogue, New York
SIZE: 2,800 square feet
ARCHITECT: John S. Whedbee
SOLAR ENGINEER: Joseph Frissora

Affording spectacular views of the ocean and bays, the house is as open to the environment as possible. For outdoor living, high decks on three sides extend from all the major rooms (see plan and views left and top). On the entry deck is a greenhouse that serves in winter as a passive collector.

ELLIOT FINE

Bold angles and an all-glass collector

Nearly four hundred vacuum tubes on the roof—like so many Thermos bottles—collect the sun's rays and act as a barrier to any heat loss.

Like a bird poised for flight, this solar house sits on a thin strip of Long Island marshland between the Atlantic Ocean and its nearby bay, soaking up solar energy through an unusual all-glass collector that sparkles in the sun. Architect John S. Whedbee designed the house for environmentalists Philip and Roslyn Barbash, who were convinced of the potential of solar energy. Their design program called not so much for an economical system as for the most advanced and efficient system appropriate for their site and comfort expectations. The bold, angular shapes of their house were designed to lean way back to catch the rays of the sun. The most striking exterior element is the collector itself, developed and manufactured by Owens-Illinois and called the SunPak.

The collector covers a 32-by-16-foot area and consists of 384 individual tube assemblies of tempered glass. Each tube is actually three in one: an outer tube, 2 inches in diameter; a black-coated intermediate tube, filled with water to be heated by the sun and returned to storage; and an inner tube that supplies fresh water from the huge, 1,000-gallon storage tank on the lowest floor of the house. Sunlight passes through the outer tube and heats water in the intermediate tube. A vacuum between these two tubes traps the heat inside—like the vacuum barrier in a Thermos bottle—virtually eliminating any conduction and convection to the outdoors. The tube assemblies join horizontal manifolds with supply and return headers, and the heat transfer medium travels through them to and from the 6-foot-diameter fiberglass tank where the heat is stored to be used for water and space heating. Because of the curved surface of the tubes, radiant energy can strike the collectors from several angles. The adjacent tube assemblies are spaced 2 inches apart to reduce the tendency of a given assembly to shade its neighbor. Near noon, when the direct radiation passes between the 2-inch tubes, spaced 2 inches apart, it hits a reflective panel behind the tube assemblies and the radiant energy bounces back through the collectors—the ricochet rays multiplying the efficiency of the system.   [*Continued*]

The living spaces of the Barbash house are as unequivocally contemporary as the energy system that heats them, with interflowing rooms, soaring spaces, interior balconies, dramatic windows and skylights. For the most efficient use of heat, the two-bedroom, two-story cedar house is divided into five separate zones. Four on the main floor are the living room, the kitchen-dining complex, the master suite, and the guest suite; the fifth, on the ground floor, is the sculpture studio, laundry, and the mechanical room for the solar system, including the computer that is keeping tabs on how it is working. Each zone has separate thermostat controls, so the owners can adjust or completely shut off the heat in zones that are not being used. Downstairs, near the storage tank, the computer that runs the zoned solar heating system has also been constantly recording all of its activities and sending the data it collects directly to an Owens-Illinois research center via the telephone wires. When the study is completed, this large, data-collecting computer will be replaced by a smaller one to continue the job of running the system.

In fireplaces, a grid of pipes carries solar system water to be heated by the fire.

ELLIOT FINE

Spiral stairs lead up to a balcony over the living room, opposite, which interflows with the dining room and shares a fireplace with it, above right. The bedrooms also have loft spaces, increasing the living and sleeping areas in the two-bedroom house.

Only a partial wall divides the kitchen from the dining room, right and below, where the soaring ceiling repeats the strong diagonal lines of the exterior. The dining area affords views out to the bay or down into the sculpture studio on the level below. A dumbwaiter carries supplies from the ground floor to the second-floor kitchen.

Active solar systems
Sun's heat empowers regional architecture

Colored like the rugged earth around it, a stucco house rises from the New Mexico landscape at one with its microclimate.

Solar collector array's strong slope is part of the drama of the design and its site.

High in the windswept mountain foothills of New Mexico, this handsome solar house is a good example of energy-conscious design in regional architecture. Architect Antoine Predock says he "wanted to create a house that would be so much at one with the New Mexico landscape that it could not exist anyplace else." Sited in a saddle of land between two hillocks, the house has a solar system that provides 80 percent of its heat in an area where the temperature often drops to 20 degrees. The architect integrated the strong slope of the solar collector array into the geometry of his design and surfaced the masonry house with light-reflecting stucco that changes color to blend with the landscape. The active solar system not only provides most heat for the house, but heats all the domestic hot water and the pool as well. The glass-faced collector panels, by Southwest Standard, cover 900 square feet of the sloping roof. A mixture of water and antifreeze flows through the black steel pipes of the heat-absorbing black steel panels, picking up the warmth from the sun and circulating it to a 6,000-gallon tank in an insulated area under the driveway for storage. Working with solar-assisted electric heat pumps, the active system added 20 percent to the initial cost of the house. The system is expected to pay for itself in fifteen years; sooner if fuel prices continue to escalate. For additional heat when it gets really cold, as it often does at this altitude, there are three fireplaces and the backup electric heat pump, which switches on to raise the temperature of the solar-heated water in the tank just enough to keep the system going.

The stucco finish on the outside of the house is applied to 8- and 16-inch-thick, insulated reinforced concrete masonry blocks — which help keep the house warm in winter and cool in summer. The floors, made of brick native to New Mexico, also absorb warmth from the low winter sun. Good natural ventilation is built in — windows catch cool air as well as dramatic views, and are sheltered to admit low winter sun, block summer sun. Natural ventilation is also induced by the stepping cross-section of the plan and high operable windows create a chimney effect. *[Continued]*

On a corner: the living room terrace.   View from entrance court side.

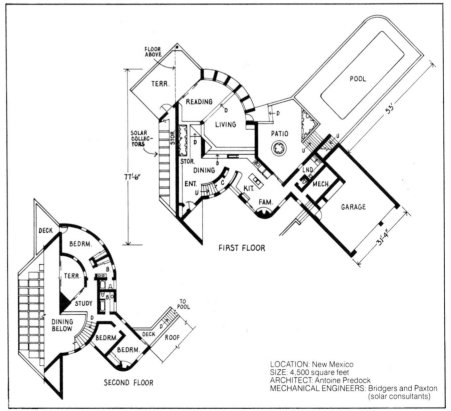

LOCATION: New Mexico
SIZE: 4,500 square feet
ARCHITECT: Antoine Predock
MECHANICAL ENGINEERS: Bridgers and Paxton
(solar consultants)

Plan shows how a variety of outdoor spaces were designed right into the house; no matter where you are inside, the outside is only steps away.

The Predock-designed house is approached via a meandering dirt road that leads to an entry court. From the court, distant views toward the west are intentionally blocked by the house but are revealed immediately upon entering. When you step inside the front door you can see through to the dining room and living areas and right out to the view terrace beyond. The rooms, like the house, step down the hillside with adjacent terraces and patios entrapping activity areas. The slant of the ceiling expresses internally the slope of the solar collector wall outside. Radial masonry walls off the living area buffer low west sun angles but permit views toward city lights at night and distant mountains. Large openings toward city views to the southwest permit the penetration of afternoon sun; the openings are protected from southerly summer sun by the outdoor deck above. The kitchen is oriented to mountain views and morning sun and connects to the outdoor court and pool entry. The sleeping zone is on the upper level, wrapping around a roof garden. The solar collector array forms a storage area and then slopes up over the entry to permit a north-oriented clerestory at the roof garden — a sort of second-floor atrium with windows that flood interior spaces on two levels with light. Breezes drift down through the roof terrace's sliding glass doors to the main level below.

From entry, a 5-foot-wide stairway curves up to roof terrace and bedrooms.

Kitchen opens to patio and pool.

Changes in levels define spaces.

Curve of sheltered glass in living area.

ELLIOTT ERWIT

Terraces surround solar-heated pool.

Three outdoor living areas serve the pool, left above. One, on main floor level, extends from the kitchen and acts as an outdoor dining room. Steps from it lead up to the pool. A second surrounds the pool itself. A third is an extension of a second-floor bedroom deck. Steps lead down from it to pool.

Water for the swimming pool is heated by the sun. With the press of a button, a black vinyl cover, left, operated by an electrically powered pulley system, extends over the pool to collect heat and prevent it from escaping when the pool is not in use.

Interior spaces make for an exciting geometry: the steep slope of the ceiling beneath the solar roof, the curve of the stairway and the window wall of the living room beyond. Dramatic vistas are revealed, above top, as the eye is led straight back through the open living spaces to the great expanses of the land behind the house. Fireplace serving both living and dining room, above center, is one of three that help heat the house on cold days.

Windows in curving living room wall, above, are deeply recessed to prevent the high summer sun from superheating the room. Floor is paved with a local terra cotta that absorbs and holds the heat of the penetrating winter sun.

In the reading area, opposite, two steps below the living room, bookshelves are built into a low partition. The interior windows overhead are those of the roof terrace.

Active solar systems

Vertical collectors outwit snow, soak up sun

On a chilly mountainside in Vermont, where the snows are heavy and the nights are cold, an exciting house draws half of its heat from the sun.

Above: progressive Victorian side of house. Opposite: the futuristic south face.

Vertical solar collectors glowing silvery in the sun soak up enough energy to provide 45 to 55 percent of the space heating and hot water for this 3,000-square-foot ski house in Vermont. Because heavy snows could overwhelm the flat plate collectors had they been placed on the roof, the collectors are mounted vertically on the south side of the house, instead of at a tilt on the roof. This atypical placement was possible because of the low winter sun angle in Vermont. With this program, designer Ric Weinschenk of Sunshine Design met a two-fold challenge presented by the site chosen for a Vermont ski house. The site has a spectacular view of the ski trail down the mountainside, but the trail is on the north, the side best left with few or no windows in a solar energy house. Rather than give up the view, the designer and clients decided to use lots of windows on the north but specified double-paned units that would be as insulative as possible. The many windows, bays, and angles give the house the appearance of a progressive Victorian farmhouse on one side; a silvery, futuristic face on the other, where 1,000 square feet of solar collectors cover most of the south façade.

There are four collector areas — two on the ground level, where the sloping land was covered with white gravel (or snow) to reflect the sun's rays into the collectors; and two on the second floor, stepped back from the shiny metal, first-floor roof, which is angled to reflect sunlight up onto the collectors. The primary heat loop of the system (activated by a differential thermostat) circulates water from the storage tank through the collectors. When the water is heated, it drops by gravity back to the storage tank. The storage tank is surrounded by Styrofoam pellets for insulation, and a heat exchanger in the tank sends preheated water to the oil burner (which acts as a backup system) for domestic radiation and domestic hot water.

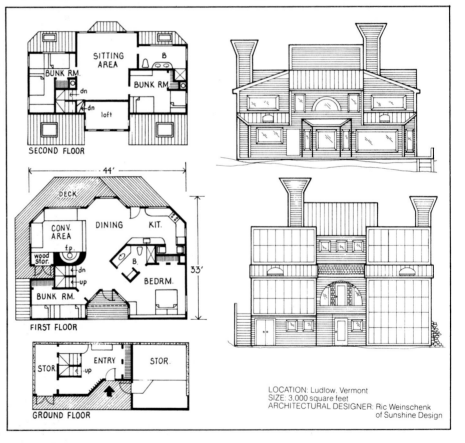

LOCATION: Ludlow, Vermont
SIZE: 3,000 square feet
ARCHITECTURAL DESIGNER: Ric Weinschenk of Sunshine Design

Master bedroom, three bunkrooms, and a loft (see plan) provide plenty of sleeping space for the owners, their four daughters, and unlimited guests. On the ground floor, storage areas and boot room open to a trail, keep winter gales out of the living areas above.

A second heat loop runs through the fireplace, opposite, below left. It can be activated by a manual switch when a fire is burning. Water from the storage tank is pumped through this secondary heat loop through part of the fireplace grating and returns heated to tank.

Living room windows, opposite, below center, look out on the trail; skylights here, and elsewhere, brighten first-floor rooms. Up in the loft, opposite, below right, windows face south, act as passive solar collectors. Loft overlooks an upstairs sitting room with spectacular views of the trail outside.

ROBERT PERRON

Active solar systems

Collectors on garage let house soar free

Detaching the garage, and confining collector panels to that roof only, frees the house to respond more completely to its inhabitants and the site around it.

Carport meets solar requirements.

One ingenious move — designing a detached garage/carport to accept flat-plate solar collectors — freed the architect of this house to design a dwelling that would be all its owners wanted it to be and all its site deserved — without ignoring the elements that would give it its energy. After finding a rare and marvelous piece of property on the California coast above San Diego, owners Andrew and Florence Cohen wanted a house with exciting spaces that would exploit their canyon site as the primary view and the sea as a secondary view. They also wanted a vital setting for living and working (Mrs. Cohen is a ceramic artist) and they wanted a house that would use solar energy. All of this was made possible by detaching the garage and confining the flat-plate collector panels to that roof only, freeing the house to respond more completely to its inhabitants and the site around it.

The long narrow three-story redwood house is inserted into the cliffs, with its windowless north side standing against the lot line. "I wanted to get it as far back as possible," architect Rob Wellington Quigley said, "to make it like a set of bleachers for looking at the cliffs." The house is designed around a linear gallery as one large open theater for living, with rooms defined by changes in level (see plan, right). The structure is further integrated with the site by a catwalk extending the linear spacial progression of the house up the canyon stream and terminating with a private sitting deck deep in the womb of the canyon.

The solar system was designed to provide 70 to 80 percent of the space heating and hot water needs of the house. It consists of 500 square feet of solar collectors and a 1,500-gallon underground storage tank connected to an "off-the-shelf" hydronic heating system. The collectors, which engineer Andrew Cohen built himself, are made of ½-inch copper tubing with aluminum fins clipped to them to absorb the sun's heat. Two sheets of fiberglass, which Mr. Cohen felt "would be lighter, cheaper and easier to work with than glass," cover the collector tubing and fins.　　　　[Continued]

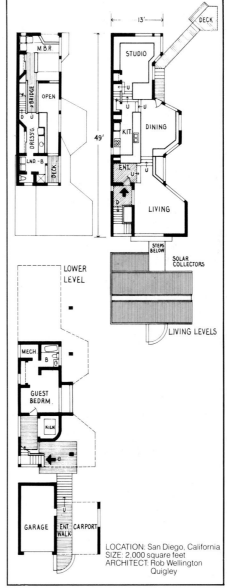

LOCATION: San Diego, California
SIZE: 2,000 square feet
ARCHITECT: Rob Wellington Quigley

The Cohen house was sited to give occupants grandstand seats for the view of a magnificent canyon. Weathering redwood siding frames glass used extensively on the south (view) side of the house. There is a minimum of glass on the north and west (windward) sides to avoid excessive heat loss. A catwalk leads to a private sitting deck at the back of the house; at the front, a high protected deck off the master bath permits spectacular views across the carport's collectors to the Pacific coast beyond.

The interiors of the Cohen house are organized by what the architect calls "successive chaos" beginning with a very neat and orderly formal entry and living room and progressing up the canyon past the centrally located dining room and kitchen to the informal "chaos" of the pottery studio. "The very sculptural interiors were not only a reaction to the site and elements," Rob Quigley says, "but also an emotional response to the work of artist Florence Cohen." In the living room, opposite, the heat stack from Mrs. Cohen's kiln comes up through the living room and is covered by extruded aluminum for a sculptural look. Upstairs, connected by a wooden foot bridge, below, the master bedroom and bath were designed as one large piece of furniture with a window seat. Throughout the house, work and living interlock and add to each other.

Interior spaces in white Sheetrock, above, are a cohesive piece of sculpture, flowing from room to room while enjoying a reasonable separation realized through half walls and cabinets that act as display spaces for the Cohen collection of art, artifacts.

Visitors coming from the enclosed entry are greeted by open spaces and spectacular views. Glass is used extensively on the south (view) side of the house, above, and where seating is close to windows thermopane was specified. The guest room on the lowest level may be thermally isolated when not in use.

Far right: The dotted line under the elevation drawing of the house shows the path of solar heat pumped into the underground storage tank, and the path of heated hot water and air out of the tank up into the house.

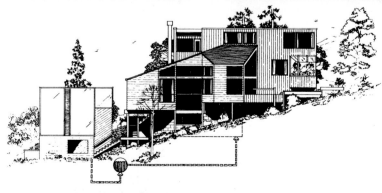

71

Low-tech system uses available parts, skills

The sun provides half of the heat and hot water needs of this mountaintop ski house built when there were few solar buildings on the horizon.

In the long-standing debate between high- and low-technology approaches to solar energy houses, this house stands as a vibrant testimony to what can be accomplished by working with the elements, with available skills, and without hard-to-get parts. Several years ago, before the wide availability of solar hardware, architect Robert F. Shannon of The People/Space Company, Boston, designed this handsome house to use the snow as well as the sun to provide a comfortable dwelling place for the Vermont skiers who inhabit it. Solar energy is collected through the south wall of the house, which includes metal-lined reflectors top and bottom, a house-wide expanse of insulated windows that catch direct sunlight, and the collector itself. Walls of the house are padded with extra insulation to hold the heat in and the roof was specially structured to hold the weight of snow, which then actually provides additional insulation when it piles up overhead.

The working south wall of the ski house has four parts. At the top, a cable-anchored, metal-lined reflector bounces sun into the house in winter or, tilted, serves as a sunshade in summer. The second section, comprised of insulated windows, brings direct sunlight into the second-story living space. The third section, the collector itself, covers the bottom third of the living room wall and an entire wall of the bottom floor below. And the fourth section, another reflector, bounces sun into the collector above, even when it is covered with snow. (This reflector is repositioned twice a year, spring and fall, to bounce the sun into the collector at the right angles as the seasons change.) Under the glass face of the collector, black-painted aluminum fins, once printing plates, absorb the sun's heat. Air soaks up the heat and transfers it to storage bins of gravel. An electric fan recirculates warm air from the bins to all the rooms. Supplemental electric heaters in the bins function when the temperature drops below a certain point. Mr. Shannon estimates that the solar elements—400 square feet of collector, 320 square feet of reflector—added about $1,000 to the cost. *[Continued]*

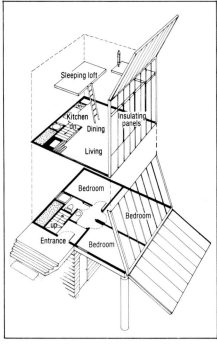

LOCATION: Vermont
SIZE: 900 square feet
ARCHITECT: Robert F. Shannon
The People/Space Company

The plan, above, places bedrooms behind the collector on the lower level; raises the living room to snare the best views along with the warmth of the sun into its one large open space. South façade, opposite, combines reflector panels, top and bottom, the collector itself, and an expansive window area, to capture as much solar energy as possible in a simple, low-tech system.

Daytime living space is one open sunny room in the 900-square-foot, Shannon-designed solar house. It is located above three bedrooms, plus entry and bath, on the level below, in a better position to capture the mountaintop views, which in Vermont roll on for miles. To keep the heat from escaping out the house-wide wall of windows—which acts as a collector by day but could be an enormous source of heat loss by night—insulating panels were built into the interior scheme. Attached to the exposed truss overhead and operating on pulleys, they can be dropped across the window wall at night to hold the day's heat in. Opposite the window wall, a Heatilator fireplace is also energy-conscious, circulating hot air back into the room rather than up the chimney. Tucked into a corner on the windowless north side of the house, the kitchen has a sleeping loft built in above it for extra guests. Downstairs there are three bedrooms, a space-conscious compartmented bath, plus an entry that confines cold air there.

The wealth of windows, blond floors and woodwork, sunny yellow furnishings, all reinforce the comfortable warm quality of the large open living space. Built-ins meet most needs; other furnishings are minimal and indestructible, but cheerful.

When all the large insulating panels are dropped down to cover the south window wall at night, they make a mural of mountains and snow to replace the real one provided by nature.

Downstairs, in one of three bedrooms, a bed hugs the collector wall, angled to catch as many of the sun's rays as possible. Below that wall, a reflector panel does its part to aid the solar collector system. Its angle can change with the angle of the sun.

Loft over kitchen sleeps guests.

Insulating panels, open and closed.

Slanting wall houses collector.

ROBERT PERRON

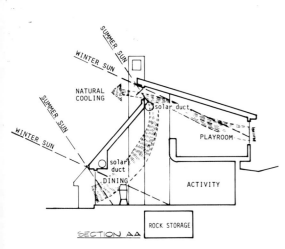

SECTION AA

SUMMER SUN
WINTER SUN
NATURAL COOLING
SUMMER SUN
WINTER SUN
solar duct
PLAYROOM
solar duct
DINING
ACTIVITY
ROCK STORAGE

Collectors, fabricated at the site, cover the long south-facing roof, above and left. Design of steep roof and of windows below allows low winter sun to enter rooms, but not the high summer sun (see diagram, left). In summer, nature does the air conditioning: North windows let in cooler air, and open clerestories let rising warm air escape.

Insulation plus the location of windows — and of the house itself — also aids climate control. The dwelling is close to the hillside, so the first 6 feet of the lower level are protected by earth.

On cold days, feeding the wood stove, opposite, is a family affair. Balconied space, opposite above, makes good use of rising hot air. Ducts are a visible part of heating scheme. On upper level (see plan) playroom and stairs separate parents' suite from children's.

Wherewithal for heating is exposed.

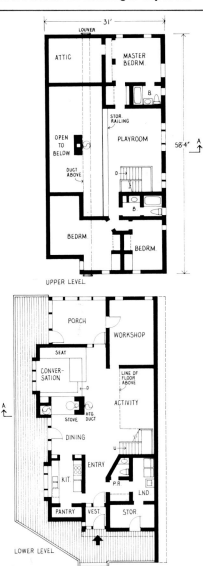

An architect's solar house, with plans you can order

Stretching across a steep site, a long house welcomes woodland views and provides enough south-facing roof for collectors.

A long expanse of flat-plate solar collectors captures the rays of the sun on the roof of this energy-conscious house; below it a south wall of glass brings in more solar heat while permitting scenic views of the woodland site. Inside, open volumes maximize the solar heat gain and share the warmth radiated by a supplemental wood stove with its flue exposed the two-story height of the house. All this works so well because when architect Robert P. Mocarsky planned a house to suit himself, wife, Lynn, and sons, Rob and Rory, an active solar system was very much part of his thinking and of the design. The family's steep, wooded property in East Hartland, Connecticut, was cooperative: Its 4½-acre slope faces south, and a picturesque brook runs near the center of the land toward the west, making it "rather easy" to orient the house to the sun as well as to brook views for major social areas.

To bring in a worthwhile amount of solar heat for the size house the family wanted, Mr. Mocarsky designed a large roof to accommodate 650 square feet of collectors on the long southwest side. To expose that expanse as much as possible, he and his wife had to cut down numerous trees. By studying the sun pattern, they were able to do so selectively. Sun-warmed air goes from the collector to ducts of a hot-air heating system. When the sun shines and rooms reach the desired temperature, the damper to the house closes and excess heat goes to a pebble bin in the crawl space for storage until needed. On days when more heat is wanted than the sun provides, electric backup equipment goes to work to help warm the rooms. Providing heat, too, of course, is the wood stove. The openness of the interior (see plans) allows several areas to share the warmth from this combined solar-electric-wood system and to share sunshine coming through downstairs windows. The domestic hot-water solar heating system is by Ford.

Mr. Mocarsky and friends made the rock bin, and much of the interior work, too, was a cooperative endeavor. Ducts, exposed primarily because the architect-owner likes having the system honestly open to view, are to be painted to accent the works. To order plans for this house, see page 144.

LOCATION: East Hartland, Connecticut.
SIZE: 2,500 square feet.
ARCHITECT: Robert P. Mocarsky

UPPER LEVEL
(Floor plan labels: LOUVER, 31', ATTIC, MASTER BEDRM., B., STOR., RAILING, OPEN TO BELOW, PLAYROOM, 58'-4", DUCT ABOVE, BEDRM., BEDRM.)

LOWER LEVEL
(Floor plan labels: PORCH, WORKSHOP, SEAT, CONVERSATION, LINE OF FLOOR ABOVE, ACTIVITY, STOVE, HTG DUCT, DINING, ENTRY, KIT., P.R., LND., PANTRY, VEST., STOR.)

Active solar systems

Technology and nature at work together

Owner-designed and owner-built, an ecology-minded Illinois house shows how technology, can be at peace with the land.

In a remarkably total approach to living with nature, this ecology-minded house is warmed by the sun in winter, cooled by natural shade and breezes in the summer. The house, designed by its owner, Mike Jantzen, has two solar heating systems built into its south side, above right. On this, the solar-energy collecting side of the house, sunlight pours through the central bubbles to warm the house directly in the cold Illinois winters. The heat of the sun is absorbed by the brick floor in the center of the living room, opposite, which returns it to the room. On each side of the bubble windows, built-in solar collectors (the stripes on the south side of the house) absorb more heat from the sun for use in the design's active solar system. The solar collectors, made from the same steel siding used to cover all the curved surfaces of the house, are painted black for better heat absorption and enclosed in fiberglass (which added the only extra cost for the collectors). The fiberglass covering traps the heat inside the collectors, which can then be pumped by a low-voltage electric blower through air ducts into rock storage under the wood floor. Water, too, is heated by the sun, through another solar collector below the center bubbles, and stored in a tank in a closet off the living room. For periods when the sun doesn't shine, there is an efficient backup system: a double combustion wood-burning stove in the living room. On a zero degree-day the airtight stove only has to be filled once to heat the house. A wood cart, designed to fit under the kitchen counter, is used to bring logs in from the wood storage area built into the north side of the house, right.

The mastermind behind this idea-filled house and its endless ingenious devices is the owner, Mike Jantzen, who calls himself a conceptual artist. He and his wife, Ellen, built the house and designed most of its furnishings. The house, constructed of wooden arches and steel siding from Republic Steel, is designed to grow. Studios for the owners, one on each end of the house, can be pulled away from the central core and more wood arches added to expand the central living space. Moreover, each section can be closed off to conserve heat and provide privacy. *[Continued]*

Blue stripes, on each side of bubble windows, identify active solar collectors.

Food pantries are built into north wall.

Brick insert in floor holds solar heat.

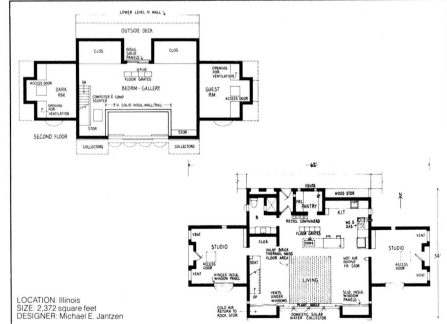

LOCATION: Illinois
SIZE: 2,372 square feet
DESIGNER: Michael E. Jantzen

On the south side of the Jantzen house, above, sunlight pours through fiberglass bubbles to warm the house directly. Collector panels on each side and under the windows absorb more heat to be used in the house's active solar system.

Inside the Jantzen house, the open central living space gathers sun not only through glass bubbles, but also through the curving translucent panels overhead, which also serve a balcony bedroom housed under the arching ceiling.

TOM YEE

The house, constructed of wooden arches and steel siding.

At each end, studios for the owners.

Nature not only warms the Jantzen house in winter but also cools it in the summer. Fresh air is kept moving by modern versions of the attic ventilator: rooftop turbine vents that pull out warm air, draw cooler air in through vents near the ground. Herbs planted in strategically placed beds, near intake vents, contribute their fragrance to freshen the air and repel insects. Under the curving roof, the bedroom is located on an open bridge above the central living space. Generous cutouts in the space open it to the living room below, the sky above. Insulated panels and Mylar flaps — the same material used by astronauts for space blankets — can close off the bedroom to provide privacy or conserve energy. The bedroom's curved walls and ceilings are foam-insulated and sprayed with a brand-new, fire-retardant wall material — Pyrocrete L/D fire-retardant foam insulation by Carboline Company. Against one pine wall, a Formica-topped plywood table has flip-up leaves that reveal storage for dishes. And when it's time to wash up, the table can be wheeled to the sink. The kitchen is outfitted with a host of energy savers. A high-pressure nozzle on the kitchen sink is gravity-fed by a water tank on the second level; a roomy Amana refrigerator runs on as much electricity as a 75-watt bulb, and a kitchen stove is run half on gas, half on wood. To see where this all began, the Jantzens' first energy-conscious house, designed and built by them, is on pages 42 through 45. Plans for either can be ordered by writing to Box 172, Carlyle, Illinois 62231. Floor plans for this house are available for $15.

Turbine vents on roof help keep air moving.

Off the upstairs bedroom, a deck among the treetops.

Bubble windows let sun in, visors keep cold out.

Under the stairs at one end of living area, a relaxation nook.

Insulated panels can close bedroom openings.

Corner kitchen with wood cart under a counter.

Bed-tent provides extra warmth, pockets add storage.

A computer in the bedroom monitors the environment.

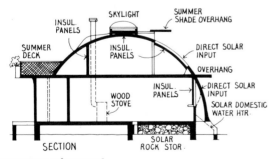

Mike Jantzen uses advanced technology to keep peace with the land. A computer can tell the occupants how the house is functioning—the temperatures inside and out, light intensity, wind stress, even sounds. This information, recorded in electrical signals, will be used to perfect all the house's energy systems, and—converted into electronic music—provide entertainment.

Active solar systems

Florida sun heats domestic hot water

Sloping forms of house hold collectors on the south, work with prevailing breezes to provide cooling, cut energy needs.

Designed to work with nature in the south of Florida, the sloping forms of this house are calculated to capture prevailing winds for natural cooling and the rays of the sun to heat domestic hot water. Architect-owner Daniel E. Adache designed the stucco over concrete block house to open to the north for exterior views of sky, water, and landscape. On that side, informal family areas open through louvered windows and sliding glass doors to lower and upper level decks that overlook a boat-filled canal. While the house opens upward and outward to north and east light, it turns its back — or its sloping roofs — to south and west, the sun exposures. These insulated roofs were designed at an appropriate angle to take solar collectors that catch the sun's rays for energy to heat domestic hot water. Four are on the roof now, but it can hold thirty. While the sun may be an adversary in the summer in Florida, Mr. Adache says, it also can be an energy saver for heating in the winter, heating domestic hot water, swimming pools, or even solar air conditioning year round. The solar collectors used in the initial phase are for heating domestic hot water only, but working with Solarcell Corporation and its concentrating collectors, Mr. Adache's long-range goal is a total solar house.

To achieve natural cooling, breezes are captured from the prevailing winds on the south side through louvered shutters and drawn through the house upward along the sloping ceilings, escaping out the other side. The high ceilings there draw the rising hot air upward, allowing the cooler, more comfortable air to remain at the living level. The goal, according to Mr. Adache, was to create a natural air-conditioning system that would capitalize on the many breezy days in Florida. On extremely hot and muggy days, an electric air-conditioning system is zoned into living and sleeping areas; at night, the air-conditioning system is directed toward the sleeping areas; in the daytime it is reversed to cool living areas. The owners estimate a saving of 30 to 50 percent of the normal usage of kilowatts for the average south Florida house of the same size. Completed in 1974, the house has been a recipient of two AIA awards and one ARA award. [*Continued*]

South roof holds collectors.

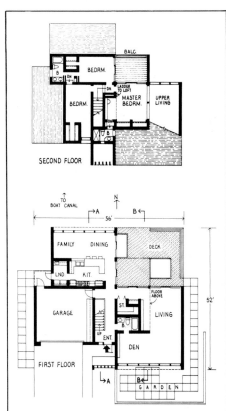

LOCATION: Fort Lauderdale, Florida
SIZE: 2,000 square feet
ARCHITECT: Daniel E. Adache

On the north, opposite, the house opens via sliding glass doors and louvered windows to views of the canal and secluded outdoor living. Plan shows living areas on the lower level, three bedrooms, two baths on the level above, a loft study at the very top.

ELLIOT FINE

The sloping forms, so important on the exterior, are experienced with equal design strength on the interior. Designed for himself, his wife, and their three children, the interior plan of the three-story house is free flowing both horizontally and vertically. Horizontally, formal and informal living areas open into one another and on outside through expansive glass walls, protected from the Florida sun by louvers, overhangs, or solar gray plate glass. Vertically, spaces also open into one another: The master bedroom overlooks the soaring living room, where a sloping ceiling takes hot air upward and out through high glass walls overhead. Wood ceiling and interior wall paneling contrast with the stucco exterior, just as lush plants provide warmth in the cool modern interiors and on the decks and patios outside. The 2,000-square-foot house has a living room, den, family room, dining room, kitchen, and utility room on the first floor; three bedrooms and two baths upstairs; and a loft over the master bedroom up under the great sloping roof.

Dining deck is on the cooler north side.

Family/dining room has walls of glass overlooking deck and canal.

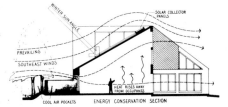

The dramatic living room, opposite, rises three stories under the great sloping roof. Glass expanse is to the north, hot air rises in this space to enhance the house's natural air-conditioning system, which brings prevailing breezes in through louvered windows on the south side; lets hot air rise and escape out north windows.

In the master bedroom, far left, a wall of sliding glass doors opens to a second-level balcony overlooking the canal. On the other side of the partial wall is the three-story-high living room.

An efficient kitchen, near left, opens to the family/dining room, divided only by a counter for informal meals. Sliding glass doors make it convenient to the deck outside.

ELLIOT FINE

Active solar systems
Engineer, architect, cooperate on design

Insulated on the outside with adobelike polyurethane foam, this Connecticut house makes exciting, visual use of its solar components on the interior.

Active solar collectors glisten on the roof of this sun-yellow house; inside, the first thing you see as you enter is a large pastel blue-gray storage tank that holds the sun's energy for future use. The owner, solar engineer Everett Barber, wanted everyone to see the size of the container needed to keep his house warm, just as he wanted to use his ideas about solar heating when it came time to build a house for his family of four. An engineer and associate professor of environmental technology, Mr. Barber asked architect Charles Moore, then a fellow teacher at Yale, to design with him a structure that would accommodate the solar heating system and contain exciting spaces made more so by the integrated solar technology.

Built on a sharp rise overlooking a salt marsh on the Connecticut shoreline, the house has most large expanses of glass facing southwest for sun and views. The roof is pitched at 57 degrees in the same direction to hold the collectors, which were mounted around two dormer windows. There are 340 square feet of collectors to gather the sun's radiation. Made by Sunworks, a company in New Haven that Mr. Barber founded, the collector design incorporates copper tubing soldered to a copper sheet under one layer of glass. Fluid in the collectors absorbs the sun's heat and carries it to the heat exchange coil in the bottom of the 2,000-gallon water storage tank in the entry. Air warmed by the tank is drawn through an insulated sleeve and moved by a fan through a blower to 30 cubic yards of 4-inch stones under the concrete floor slab. Air is forced through the rocks up to perimeter floor registers.

The rock storage area also contains heat gained from a unique method of house-heat recovery developed by Everett Barber. Normal house heat—generated during the day by window heat gain, use of the kitchen and fireplace, and by the activity of occupancy itself — rises through an open, double-height living room to the top of the house. There a return-air duct draws the heat out of the space and diverts it around the solar heat storage tank into the rock storage area under the concrete floor.

Ducts, flues, tank seen from belvedere.

Kitchen storage, too, is open to view.

Fireplace flue, warm-air duct exposed.

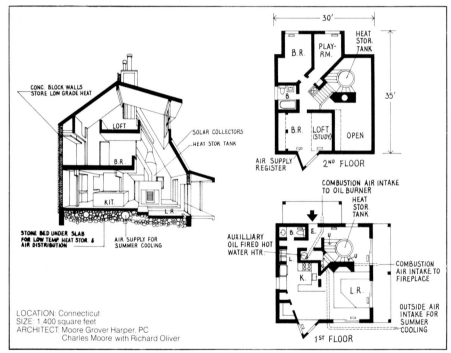

CONC. BLOCK WALLS STORE LOW GRADE HEAT

LOFT

B.R.

KIT.

SOLAR COLLECTORS

HEAT STOR. TANK

L.R.

STONE BED UNDER SLAB FOR LOW TEMP HEAT STOR. & AIR DISTRIBUTION

AIR SUPPLY FOR SUMMER COOLING

30'

B.R. | PLAY-RM. | HEAT STOR. TANK

35'

B.R. | LOFT (STUDY) | OPEN

AIR SUPPLY REGISTER

2ND FLOOR

COMBUSTION AIR INTAKE TO OIL BURNER

HEAT STOR. TANK

AUXILLIARY OIL FIRED HOT WATER HTR.

K.

L.R.

COMBUSTION AIR INTAKE TO FIREPLACE

OUTSIDE AIR INTAKE FOR SUMMER COOLING

1ST FLOOR

LOCATION: Connecticut
SIZE: 1,400 square feet
ARCHITECT: Moore Grover Harper, PC
Charles Moore with Richard Oliver

Eight-inch-thick concrete block walls add a passive aspect to the solar house, opposite. They absorb heat from the sun's rays and radiate it any time air inside is at a lower temperature than the walls. Four inches of sprayed and sealed polyurethane foam on the outside of the walls insulate this thermal mass and seal the edges of door and window openings. Polyurethane foam on the exterior of the house was painted yellow with Thoroseal paint, which, with concrete in it, gives the foam some required fire protection. Porch roof and dormer overhangs keep out sun's heat in summer, let it in during the winter.

Steps to second floor wind between heat storage tank and back of large stone fireplace, right, where a heat absorber helps heat water in the storage tank. Tank is painted blueish-gray in keeping with the pastel colors in the rest of the house. Each wall is a different shade, chosen by consultant Tina Beebe from a Turner watercolor.

ROBERT PERRON

INSULATING GLASS

FUTURE INSULATING CURTAIN

WIND BRACE

DEC. 21 ALTITUDE

FLAT PLATE COLLECTORS

PLEXIGLAS

CL.

BEDRM.

LIVING

KIT.

SECTION

ROBERT PERRON

High glass on south is trap for sun's heat.

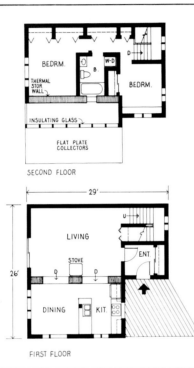

LOCATION: Waitsfield, Vermont
SIZE: 1,244 square feet
ARCHITECTS: Circus Studios, Ltd.
SOLAR CONSULTANTS: Doug Taft/Gardenway Laboratories
Bryan Burke

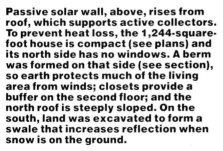

Passive solar wall, above, rises from roof, which supports active collectors. To prevent heat loss, the 1,244-square-foot house is compact (see plans) and its north side has no windows. A berm was formed on that side (see section), so earth protects much of the living area from winds; closets provide a buffer on the second floor; and the north roof is steeply sloped. On the south, land was excavated to form a swale that increases reflection when snow is on the ground.

Wide overhangs in the thick thermal wall allow air to circulate between the living room, opposite far left, step-down kitchen, opposite near left, and adjoining dining room, right. Extra light comes through glass overhead.

Concrete, plus glass, soaks up solar heat

With tons of masonry to absorb warmth, and solar collectors for hot water, a hybrid system helps conserve fossil fuel in Vermont.

Active and passive collectors absorb the sun's rays on the south wall and roof of this hybrid solar house built on flat land in Waitsfield, Vermont, as a solar demonstration project. To help keep rooms warm in winter, passive elements in the design include thick masonry, triple glazing for all operable windows, extra insulation, an earth berm on the windowless north side, and a south wall specially engineered to soak up solar heat. "Left to its own means, the house can collect, store, and radiate warmth from the sun," says Ted Montgomery of Circus Studios, architect of the two-story structure.

The active system, included to help heat water for domestic use, has 76 square feet of collectors on a south-facing roof. The passive solar south wall is made of heavy-weight aggregate concrete blocks stained dark brown to increase absorption of the sun's rays. About 4 feet out from the specially designed wall, on the upper level, a second wall of insulating glass was built to keep the heat in. Space between the glass and masonry walls allows for a skylight to brighten the rooms below. Within the 16-inch-thick block walls are ducts for a hot-air heating system. Air in the ducts picks up heat from the sun-warmed wall before going to a gas-fired furnace. If the air is warm enough, it can be circulated as is; if not, the furnace goes on and boosts the temperature. The architects advocate wood stoves as the first backup, and one stove was recently installed in the living room. The solar heating system is working well: A tankful of propane gas (250 gallons, $130), put in last May had not been used up by January, and wood was burned mostly for its aesthetic effect.

For cool interiors in summer, a fan in the north roof near the peak pulls hot air out of the attic area and the space between block wall and glass. An insulating curtain can shade the south wall by day. The house was built by Greenmoss Builders, Inc., with the aid of a grant under the residential solar demonstration program of the U.S. Department of Housing and Urban Development. In both the domestic hot water and space heating systems, the aim was for solar energy to provide about 50 percent of the fuel needs.

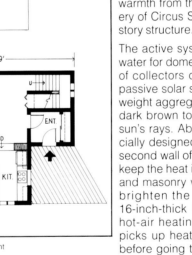

Active solar systems

A village of solar-heated houses

From California to Cape Cod, solar communities are being developed with houses sited to use the sun.

One of a growing number of developments of solar-heated houses in the United States, Snow Pond Village on Cape Cod, Massachusetts, is planned to include over fifty houses that look to the sun for their major source of energy. Snow Pond Village houses, designed by Add, Inc., of Cambridge, Massachusetts, reflect the traditional forms and materials of New England saltboxes and Cape Cod houses. The steeply pitched roofs of these familiar housing forms lend themselves well to the requirements of solar collectors and they have been designed to incorporate active solar systems that are expected to provide 65 percent of the space heating requirements and 75 percent of the hot water requirements.

The active solar system consists of 380 square feet of copper collectors by Kennecott Copper located within the structure of the roof. Water is pumped through the system, heated, and stored in an insulated 2,225-gallon tank in the basement. The heat gathered in the water is transferred to a conventional forced-air distribution system with registers located throughout the house. The system will deactivate and drain down when the collector temperatures drop below 90 degrees Fahrenheit to prevent freezing and conserve the heat in the tank. If the temperature of the water in the tank drops below a certain point, a backup electric coil will be activated to supplement the system. The domestic hot water system also takes heat from the solar tank and has a similar backup heat source.

Houses are sited so that collectors are facing 10+ degrees due south. The active areas of the house — living and dining rooms — also face south and have large window openings to take advantage of passive solar heat gain. More functional areas, such as stairways and baths, are on the north side of the house, where window openings are kept small to minimize heat loss. The Snow Pond Village houses are heavily insulated: R-21 at the walls, an average of R-25 at the roof areas.

The Snow Pond Village houses, two-, three-, and four-bedroom models, can be purchased with or without the solar system, which adds $9,000 to the cost of the three-bedroom model.

On the north, windows are minimal to minimize heat loss.

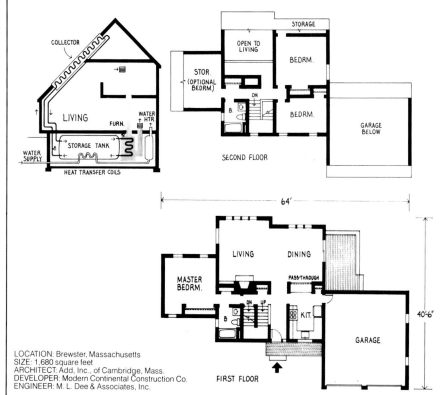

LOCATION: Brewster, Massachusetts
SIZE: 1,680 square feet
ARCHITECT: Add, Inc., of Cambridge, Mass.
DEVELOPER: Modern Continental Construction Co.
ENGINEER: M. L. Dee & Associates, Inc.

Saltbox angles are right for collectors.

Cedar clapboards sheath the exterior of the model house at Snow Pond Village, and textured asphalt shingles surround the copper collectors on the south-facing roof, opposite. Windows on this exposure are larger to take advantage of passive solar heat gain; all windows have double glazing.

Living area, opposite below, has a cathedral ceiling rising to a second-level balcony overlooking the space. Plan, above, is of the three-bedroom model, with a two-car garage, sundeck.

STEVE ROSENTHAL

Active solar houses

A great sloping roof holds many collectors

Built on speculation, this solar energy house may be the forerunner of what more and more energy-conscious house shoppers will be offered.

This handsome house, with its dramatic sloping roof housing low-profile collectors, reveals how a solar energy design can accommodate all the features that would appeal to prospective suburban home buyers. The builders of the house, built on speculation in suburban New York, were John Reventas and Carlo Ventimiglia, who decided the time had come to step up the future a bit. Very much aware of the advances in solar energy technology as well as fuel prices, they were interested in the possibilities of having the sun help heat the houses they build in the northern clime of suburban New York. They turned to the architectural firm of Raymond, Rado, Caddy, and Bonnington, asking for a design incorporating a solar energy system but with the kind of generous plan that would appeal to a wide spectrum of prospective homeowners. They also wanted to use their usual labor force to build the house and they wanted to work with readily available components.

Architect Howard Bonnington's solution utilizes a great sloping roof, large enough to accommodate twenty-four flat-plate solar collectors. Under that sloping roof, two floors of living space provide all the amenities for comfortable living. Within the house, ductwork as well as plumbing is conventional, so there are no strange elements exposed to the interior spaces that flow from one another and to a deck that is also housed within the broad outlines of the strong exterior silhouette. The exterior combines such simple materials as textured plywood siding and concrete block, all familiar to the crew that built the house. At least half the heating needs of the 2,400-square-foot structure are met by energy supplied by the sun. Sealed within the aluminum collectors, by General Energy Devices, Inc., is a transfer fluid that, when heated by the sun, flows through an integral pattern of channels, then to piping systems for forced-warm-air heating and domestic hot water. The house faces a little west of due south for prolonged exposure to direct rays after collectors have been warmed by morning sun. For optimum efficiency, too, the roof has a 50-degree slope and insulation is extra heavy.

Balcony is set into collector array.

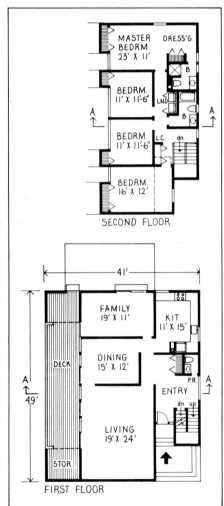

SECOND FLOOR

MASTER BEDRM. 23' X 11' DRESS'G.
BEDRM. 11' X 11'-6"
BEDRM. 11' X 11'-6"
BEDRM. 16' X 12'

FIRST FLOOR

41'
49'
FAMILY 19' X 11' KIT 11' X 15'
DECK
DINING 15' X 12'
ENTRY
LIVING 19' X 24'
STOR.

LOCATION: New Castle, New York
SIZE: 2,400 square feet
ARCHITECTS: Raymond, Rado, Caddy, and Bonnington
SYSTEM DESIGN: General Energy Devices, Inc.

HOWARD BONNINGTON

Built on a one-acre hillside site, the setting for the house, above, was left as natural as possible; only sun-blocking trees were removed. Driveway to the property is over a small stream, above left.

The plan of the house, left, concentrates formal and informal living areas on the lower level, bedrooms and baths on the floor above. Both the living and dining rooms open to a large deck, while the family room opens on grade to an adjacent terrace. The lowest level includes space for a studio/recreation room, the garage, plus a mechanical room for the water storage tank, heat distribution equipment, backup oil and electrical systems.

Confined within the sloping, south-facing roof, large windows, above, are set back to capture low sun in winter, exclude summer sun. Collectors are attached above the roof on this same south-facing elevation (see right). Heated fluid from most collectors (A, diagram far right) goes to a 3,700-gallon storage tank (D) in the basement. The stored energy provides heat for a conventional forced-air system. Other collectors (B) provide heat for domestic hot water. Whenever reservoir temperature is too low, the appropriate standby heat goes on, electric for domestic hot water, oil for space heating.

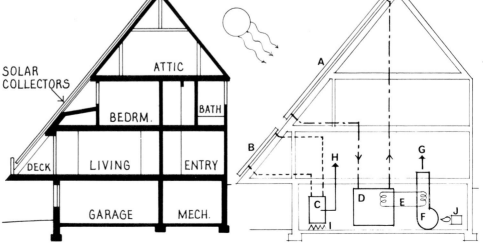

SOLAR COLLECTORS

ATTIC

BEDRM.

BATH

DECK   LIVING   ENTRY

GARAGE   MECH.

A

B

H

C   I

D   E   G   F   J

ROBERT PERRON

Sixteen Grumman Sunstream collectors, above, provide 400 square feet of effective solar energy collection at a 45-degree angle on the roof. Collectors face 20 degrees west of south to effectively bias the system toward the afternoon sun.

On the interior, right and above right, insulated shutters keep heat in, cold out. Heat loss from the 2,300-square-foot house has been as minimal as the design team estimated, and the solar system provides 55 percent of the heating requirements.

Fireplace design provides heat gain.

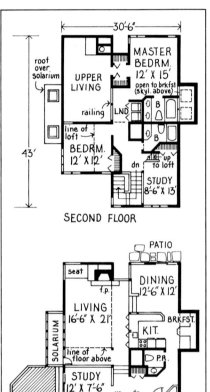

SECOND FLOOR

30'-6"

43'

roof over solarium

UPPER LIVING

MASTER BEDRM. 12' X 15'

open to brkfst (skyl. above)

railing

line of loft

LND

B

B

B

BEDRM. 12' X 12'

up to loft

dn

STUDY 8'-6" X 13'

FIRST FLOOR

PATIO

seat

f.p.

DINING 12'-6" X 12'

LIVING 16'-6" X 21'

SOLARIUM

line of floor above

BRKFST.

KIT.

P.R.

DECK

STUDY 12' X 7'-6"

up

dn

ENT.

ST.

LOCATION: Quechee, Vermont
SIZE: 2,440 square feet
ARCHITECTURAL DESIGNER: Blue Minges

The house was designed with an open plan, above, and all ductwork and plumbing are contained in one central core. Double entry prevents warm air from escaping during opening and closing of the outside door.

Designed to catch and conserve sun's energy

A cedar-sided house in Vermont utilizes energy-conservation techniques to make the most of the heat it gathers from the sun.

The success of the energy system in this Vermont house is credited as much to energy-conservation techniques as it is to the design and sizing of the solar hardware it uses to capture energy from the sun. Designer Blue Minges of Farmington, Connecticut, and builder-owner Robert Terrosi of Quechee, Vermont, wanted to develop "a structure which through its design achieves maximum comfort with the least amount of purchased energy." To do this they employed considerable energy-conservation features to lower the house's energy needs. By using post and beam construction, the walls could have their siding applied, then sprayed with 1¾ inches of urethane, which would then act as structural sheathing as well as insulation. This put insulation on the outside of the house and sealed walls against air infiltration. Other major energy savers include Andersen triple-glazed windows with sealed gas sandwich; an entrance alcove to prevent warm air escape; a solarium with insulated shutters to accept solar input during the day, prevent loss at night; and no windows on the insulated masonry north wall, which absorbs heat during the day and radiates it at night. Solarium and 8-inch-thick masonry north wall act as passive solar collectors.

The active solar system utilizes sixteen Sunstream solar collectors from Grumman Energy Systems, providing 400 square feet of effective area. Mounted on the roof, the plastic panels are curved to keep off snow. The collector was sized to meet midseason requirements, rather than the worst winter conditions, which in Quechee can mean −30 degrees Fahrenheit. Nearly 100 percent of the heating requirement is satisfied by the solar system during a significant portion of the year, 55 percent overall. The water-to-air heat pump system is backed up by an oil burner, a choice that was made because it would give the owner an energy source independent from the utility system with its primarily nuclear source of energy. The system splits the risk of rising prices between two entirely different fuel sources, and there is a limited amount of flexibility so that the homeowner can favor one system or the other as fuel costs change.

Demonstration houses

Conceived to show solar use for today

Part of OMSI Energy Center, Tera One is a research house that demonstrates and monitors energy-saving devices that are available to the public now.

Built as a laboratory for energy-conservation ideas, this house, designed by Skidmore, Owings, and Merrill, is expected to save at least 50 percent in energy use compared to a similar-sized 1,500-square-foot house without its features. Dominating the exterior of the house is a steeply sloping solar collector wall on the south side. With an array of nine air-type solar collector panels covering its central portion, that same wall, opposite, reveals two passive energy-collecting features of the house: a greenhouse off the living room that is part of the heating/cooling system, and louvers over bedroom windows that provide shade in summer and allow the sun in during winter months. The house, called Tera One, for Total Energy Resource Application, was developed as a research facility by the Pacific Power and Light Company and built on land provided by the city of Portland near the Oregon Museum of Science and Industry. There it serves as a showcase of energy-conservation ideas currently available to the public and as a research-gathering data bank for the sponsoring utility. Designed for a family of four, the house seems more complex than it is because of a sophisticated computer that is constantly tracking the amount of solar radiation and performance of the solar system.

Tera One's active solar system utilizes traditional flat-plate collectors. The 185-square-foot collector area, angled at 70 degrees from horizontal, absorbs heat from solar radiation that is then drawn off by mechanical fans and moved into the house or placed in storage. The design and specifications for the house recognize the importance of cutting down on energy requirements. Incorporated in it are several methods of insulation so comparisons can be made. Oversized wood members provide exceptional space for loose bulk insulating materials in most exterior wall framing; other walls are insulated with mineral blanket or foam, the foundation with insulated foam board. Kitchen and laundry appliances were chosen for energy efficiency. A heat-reclaiming system extracts heat from dishwater and clothes wash water that is then used to help preheat the house's hot water supply.

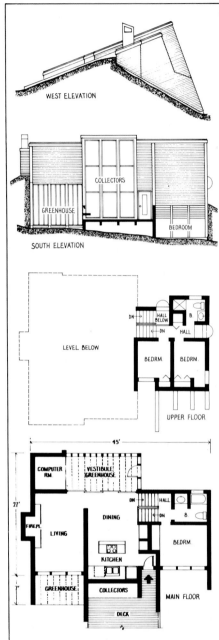

WEST ELEVATION

COLLECTORS
GREENHOUSE
BEDROOM
SOUTH ELEVATION

LEVEL BELOW
HALL BELOW
DN
DN
HALL
B.
BEDRM.
BEDRM.
UPPER FLOOR

COMPUTER RM.
VESTIBULE GREENHOUSE
DN
HALL
B.
FIREPL.
LIVING
DINING
BEDRM.
KITCHEN
GREENHOUSE
COLLECTORS
MAIN FLOOR
DECK

LOCATION: Portland, Oregon
SIZE: 1,250 square feet
ARCHITECT: Skidmore, Owings, and Merrill

Built up as a berm against some outside walls and covering the top of a portion of the north-facing roof, right, earth is also used as an insulating material. The building surface was reduced through partial two-story construction, and the house makes extensive use of natural western wood products, chosen for their energy-conservation qualities. A vestibule at the north-side front door cuts down on outside air infiltration.

The building (see plans and elevations above) was designed to minimize space heating requirements. Somewhat minimal glazing is maximized by interior openings that allow light to spill from one area into another.

One wall of the living room, far left, is a greenhouse, which also collects solar heat in the winter. Plants, through the natural process of giving off water vapor, become part of the cooling system in the summer. The fireplace relies on outside air for combustion; a glass screen prevents warm air from being used in the process. Louvers are angled to provide shade in summer, allow the sun in during winter months.

A house to showcase the sun's power

Energy from the sun not only warms but also cools this desert house, plus powers the stereo system and locks the front door.

The Copper Development Association's Decade 80 Solar House was designed to showcase the energy-conserving technology that is now available. Built in Tucson, Arizona, in 1975 to demonstrate the practical value of sun power as an alternate energy source, the house has an overall climate control system by Arkla Industries that not only provides almost 100 percent of the space heating requirements, but cools it in summer as well. The sun's energy also heats the domestic hot water, powers the stereo system, and even locks the front door. A small separate solar system, utilizing silicon photovoltaic cells, converts the sun's energy directly to low-voltage power for selected uses. Electric power for lighting, cooking, and appliances is utility-supplied.

Architect M. Arthur Kotch conceived the house as a desert compound, combining a series of units (see plan), each roofed with copper laminated to plywood panels. The north as well as the south slopes of the roof are covered with the copper-laminated panels, but only the south-facing panels act as energy collectors. The collector panels consist of 2-by-8-foot copper sheets and rectangular copper tubes fastened to them, both blackened for maximum absorbing power. Although photographed without them, the panels are normally covered with glass to trap the solar heat hitting the collectors. Radiant heat trapped in the collectors is transferred to water in the tubes and circulated by pumps into a storage tank. This energy then is transferred as needed (via ITT Bell and Gossett heat exchangers, pumps, and control valves) to an absorption chiller or to a fan coil unit for cooling or heating the house (see diagram). Fiberglass ducts provide noiseless distribution of warm and cool air from the Arkla units. According to the Copper Development Association, 98.7 percent of the space heating, as well as heating for the domestic hot water, is supplied by the system. Heating needs are less in Tucson than in most parts of the country, but cooling demands are greater, so the house was designed, insulated, and glazed with cooling in mind. [*Continued*]

The house was designed as a copper-roofed desert compound.

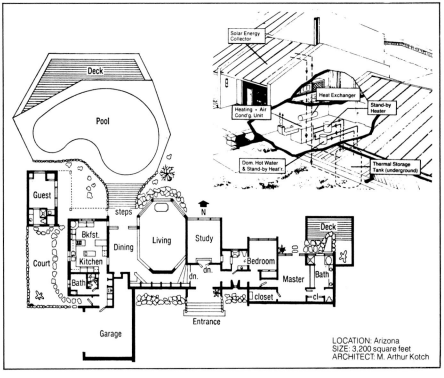

LOCATION: Arizona
SIZE: 3,200 square feet
ARCHITECT: M. Arthur Kotch

Because cooling is more of a problem than heating in Tucson, where temperatures can soar to 120 degrees Fahrenheit, there are few openings on the hot south side. The great expanses of glass, opposite, on the north-facing side are made of a special bronze-insulated glass that reduces heat gain or loss to half that experienced with clear, single-pane glass. The same glass is used on either side of the copper-clad front door, right.

The pool, above, is also temperature controlled by solar energy. Chlorinated water is pumped through the tubing of solar panels that make up a separate system on the cabana roof for heating or cooling the water in the pool.

HORST

98

The interiors of the house, designed by
Ving Smith and Charlotte Smith, take
their cue from the desert environment.
Wood beams span a sky blue ceiling in
the living room, above and left, with
areas for living and dining defined by a
change in floor levels.

The same blue of the living room ceiling
is seen in the bower of Batik sheeting
from Burlington in the master bedroom,
right. Furnishings here, and most of
those throughout the house, are by
Burlington Industries.

Kitchen/breakfast area has cozy hearth.

The Decade 80 Solar House is one of the few houses known that gets some of its electrical power from the sun. In addition to the sun-powered climate-control systems, the house contains a small separate system directly converting solar energy to electrical energy. Silicon photovoltaic cells, mounted on the master bathroom roof, convert the sun's energy directly to low-voltage power for selected uses. This permits some of the small low-voltage appliances in the kitchen of the house to get their power from the sun in the same way an orbiting spacecraft does. The silicon cells, developed by Solar Power Corporation, collect solar energy to be stored in batteries in the basement energy room. Electrical wiring carries the power to certain outlets in the house, to be used for any appliance that can be run on batteries — a small TV, the kitchen clock. Solar cells also run the electronic lock for the front door, and provide standby power for an electrical energy security system.

HORST

In the den, above, and throughout the house, Scotchgard Brand Fabric Protectors from the 3M Company keep upholstery, draperies, and wall coverings fresh-looking and soil-free. All draperies in the house are woven of Owens-Corning Fiberglas yarn.

Accessible only from the master bath, right, is a secluded sundeck for private enjoyment of the sun. Fencing and decking are of garden grades of California redwood. A mirrored copper wall in the bathroom brings the copper of the exterior inside. Tub and lavatories are by American Standard.

In the family room/kitchen, above left and center, energy-saving appliances include Amana's Radarange microwave oven, which cuts energy consumption, and an energy-saving refrigerator that uses only 2.9 kilowatt-hours of electricity per day — little more than a single 100-watt light bulb.

Decade 80 Solar House participating sponsors: Amana Refrigeration, American Standard, Arkla Industries, Burlington Industries, California Redwood Association, Cascade Industries, ITT Bell and Gossett, Jenn-Air Corporation, the Maytag Company, Owens-Corning Fiberglas Corporation, PPG Industries, Schlage Lock Company, Tile Council of America, 3M Company, and U.S. Plywood Division of Champion International Corporation.

101

Demonstration houses

RIT research project leads to building a solar house

In Rochester, New York, where the sun gets through the clouds only 54 percent of the time, an Energy House was built to demonstrate solar power.

This solar-powered contemporary saltbox on the Rochester Institute of Technology (RIT) campus was designed to test the feasibility of getting substantial amounts of the house's space heating and domestic hot water requirements from the sun. Built in western New York, where the sun gets through the clouds only 54 percent of the time, the Energy House grew out of research by RIT faculty member Dr. Paul Wojciechowski. Using historical weather data to model the house on a computer before it was built, his research indicated it would be feasible to use the sun's energy for power in what many consider a far from ideal solar climate. Early reports on the house's operation indicate that his predictions — more than half the space and hot water heating from the sun — are on target.

The house was designed by architect John Fayko, with a cubic shape that cuts down on the exterior area exposed to the wind and minimal use of windows on the north, east, and west sides. The traditional, steeply pitched roof offers the perfect surface for the thirty-eight solar collectors that transform the sun's rays into heat. To efficiently use Rochester's winter sun, the roof is angled at 60 degrees so that the sun's rays are nearly perpendicular to the solar panels during the most demanding heating period.

The solar design includes both flat-plate and tubular collectors, as well as the passive advantages of a wide expanse of southern windows, which let the winter sun flood directly into the 1,832-square-foot house. Within the active solar collection system there are two separate solar loops: one for space heating, the other for domestic hot water. The more elaborate system is for space heating and utilizes thirty-six Sunworks copper flat-plate liquid collectors. Four 1,000-gallon water tanks in the basement store the sun's heat. (When temperatures in storage drop below 95 degrees, the water bypasses the system's heat exchange coil and goes to an electric heat pump instead.) The domestic hot-water solar loop uses two KTA tubular collectors mounted on the garage roof.

Sun shines on south-facing collector.

Roofs hold flat and tubular collectors.

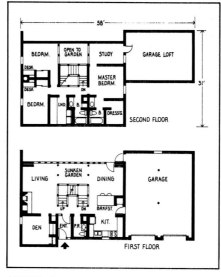

LOCATION: Rochester, New York
SIZE: 1,832
ARCHITECT: John Fayko
SOLAR CONSULTANT: Paul Wojciechowski

ROBERT PERRON

Few interior walls and a two-and-a-half-story atrium (see plans above and photos opposite below) permit the sun's heat and light to reach throughout the house. A 39-inch overhang keeps the sun out during summer months, when it isn't needed.

The Energy House was built as a cooperative project of RIT, Rochester Gas and Electric Corporation, and the Rochester Home Builders' Association.

Windows in the Energy House, above, are triple paned. Framing is 2-by-6s on 24-inch centers to allow for 6 inches of fiberglass batting insulation. Under the cedar clapboards, the house is sheathed with 1-inch styrofoam.

ROBERT ROSE

Underground houses

For a variety of environmental reasons, a small group of innovative architects is now designing underground houses, and there is a natural alliance between underground construction and energy-conscious architecture. Properly constructed, underground houses are energy-efficient in themselves, and with the inclusion of south-facing glass areas, they can collect, absorb, and release the sun's rays to help in the heating. Solar gain through windows and skylights, preserved within by the blanket of surrounding earth, can be sufficient to keep the inside temperature in the 70-degree range while the sun is out. This is true because 5 feet down, below the frost level, the earth's temperature is a relatively constant 54 degrees, impervious to sleet, hail, cold winds, or broiling sun. Whether the requirement is for heating or cooling, the underground house has a head start. It takes less energy to keep a house at 68 degrees when it is surrounded by a 54-degree earth blanket than when it sits aboveground in temperatures below zero or in the 90s.

While the earth is an excellent moderator of temperature fluctuations, it is not a good insulator. Insulation inside and out helps prevent heat loss in underground houses. Roofs of underground houses must be carefully designed, of course, to accommodate the extraordinary weight of earth, plants, and sometimes trees, ranging from 150 pounds per square foot to 400.

Obviously, houses can only be built below grade where soil conditions permit. Percolation and drainage tests must be taken by competent engineers. When the water table is too high, or the site is on fill, the house can be constructed above grade and bermed all around. This simpler method — earth berms used to partially cover exterior walls — may have both cost and aesthetic advantages on sloping sites.

On the following eight pages, you will see several examples of designs built into the earth with insulated concrete walls that absorb and store the sun's heat gathered through exposed walls of south-facing glass. Skylights or shed-roofed light wells, set into sod roofs, bring light into the more recessed areas of some of these underground houses and aid in their ventilation. These houses, protected from daily temperature fluctuations because of their blankets of surrounding earth, have exceptional thermal momentum to store heat from day to night, or, in warmer climates, to keep them a pleasant 70 degrees Fahrenheit even on the warmest of days.

ELLIOTT ERWIT

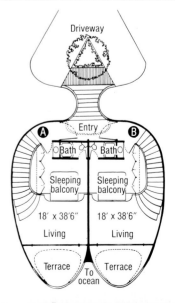

104

Underground houses
Earth shields a double beach house

Not unlike concrete eggshells in form, a two-unit house is closely linked to nature under a thick layer of sodded earth which aids temperature moderation.

A fascinating example of organic architecture, this sod-roofed beach house appears to grow out of the Florida dunes. The unique earth house was designed by architect William Morgan to share a site with his own high-reaching cedar house, and it was not to disturb his ocean view. The architect-owner buried the building in a dune formed by erosion in a 1960s hurricane. The earth has proven a good moderator of nature's temperature fluctuations. Inside temperature, thanks to the blanket of earth, is a constant 70 degrees Fahrenheit, though some heat gain is observed in the morning. Morning sunlight comes through the sliding glass doors that open the back of the building, which faces east, to spectacular views of the Atlantic Ocean. This light, as well as ocean glare, is controlled with reflective blinds.

The residence was planned with computer help in siting and building. Mr. Morgan consulted with engineers at Geiger-Berger, and their use of a computer at Columbia University helped determine the eggshell shape. Although Mr. Morgan and Geiger-Berger tested hypothetical shapes and mapped areas of stress with computer efficiency, the human component remained vital. The designers rejected the first two computer solutions, choosing the third shape that the computer proved sound. The framing system was based on the theory that a thin-skinned curve, like the shell of an egg, would distribute weight equally. Gunite, a cement without aggregate often used for free-form swimming pools, was chosen to form the structural shell, and the earth surrounding the structure would also help distribute the load evenly and would moderate temperatures effectively. The building began with excavation. Then the lower part of the structure was built much like a swimming pool — a 4-inch slab bounded by a vertical wall. This lower wall carries steel reinforcing bars that were bent to become basic members of the dome form. This form was then built up with metal lath, sprayed with a thin layer of concrete to thicken and rigidify the form and to serve as a base for the sprayed Gunite of the structural shell. After two weeks of curing, the shell was waterproofed, sand loaded back on top, and sod was planted over all. Under the sod there are two identical living units.

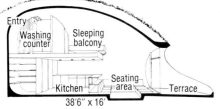

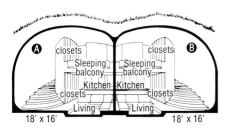

LOCATION: Atlantic Beach, Florida
SIZE: 750 square feet, each unit
ARCHITECT: William Morgan Architects

The living rooms of this pair of apartments built into a Florida dune are opened up by big "eyes" on the ocean side, above, leading to sheltered terraces that capture the sun on their white, curving walls.

Entries on the upper level (see plans and sections, left) lead to a bath and a sleeping balcony that overlooks the living room of each unit reached by a stairway that sweeps down from street level above, or from the terrace.

ROBERT PERRON

A postmodernist porch roof shades the exposed south-facing wall of an underground house, above, in summer, but allows the sun's rays to heat the passive solar house in fall and winter.

The energy-independent mountain retreat has a clapboard façade, structural concrete walls that absorb and store heat, and interiors finished in local pine boards, left.

Compact rooms (see plan above right and photos left) open one into another, sharing space and views but providing functional divisions. Walls of glass not only bring in the sun but provide spectacular vistas of Vermont's Green Mountains some 40 miles away.

The underground house has good ventilation, assisted by skylights set in the 18-inch sod roof.

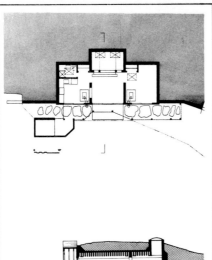

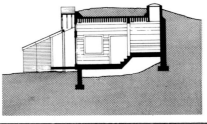

LOCATION: Vermont
SIZE: 600 square feet
ARCHITECT: Mark Simon of Moore Grover Harper, PC

Bermed walls hold heat from the sun

Built into the earth, insulated concrete walls absorb and store the sun's heat gathered by a wall of south-facing glass.

Set into the side of a large open hill, the only exposed wall of this small Vermont house faces a southerly direction, allowing the sun to heat it in fall, winter, and spring. Extremely well-insulated concrete walls, protected by the earth, give the house exceptional thermal momentum to store heat from day to night. Rear walls of insulated concrete are set deep into the earth, which has a constant temperature of 54 degrees, even in coldest winter. From its house-wide porch there are grand vistas out to the Green Mountains 40 miles away. The porch roof shades the expanse of glass in summer and centers on a decorative gable, which, according to the architect, Mark Simon, "reassures any nervous occupants that they are still in a house like the nearby Greek Revival and Victorian homesteads of the area."

The house has a deep sod roof with 18 inches of earth on top that hide it from view farther up the hill. Thus the architect met the owners' wishes for a mountain retreat that would blend into its site — a hill and large open field overlooking a central Vermont valley. Joan and David Crowell wanted an "ecological" energy-independent house. Because their children were grown, the plan requirements could be minimal: one master bedroom, one bath, a kitchen, one living/dining area, one living/sleeping alcove, one storage/generator shed (see plan, left). The passive solar house that Mark Simon designed for them has exceptional energy-conservation qualities. In addition to the 18-inch-deep sod roof, the structural concrete walls are insulated on the outside, permitting them to absorb and store the heat from the sun coming through the south-facing glass. Last winter, with temperatures going to minus 25 degrees, the house, unheated, went below 32 degrees only once. The only backup heating is supplied by two wood stoves. The house stays cool and dry in summer with good ventilation through the four skylights. Water is supplied without pumps by natural pressure from underground springs up the hill. Lights run on bottled gas. Someday they will be replaced by ones powered by a wind generator, "which will take advantage of the local abundance of that natural power source," the architect says.

107

Underground houses

Sod-roof house dug into a hillside

With temperature changes moderated by the earth, this masonry house is warm in the winter and cool in the summer.

Designed with a deeply inset south-facing wall of glass to collect the sun's energy, built with structural concrete walls to absorb and store the sun's heat, and pocketed in the earth with a layer of sod overhead to further insulate it, here is a house conceived to work with nature. For years, designer Don Metz had had the urge to build a house with a sod roof. Then he found the perfect site: an Alpine sort of pasture near the top of a small mountain in New Hampshire. The design he had in mind, Mr. Metz explains, had to "be built on a hillside with a southern view, and should be only one-story high." The exterior of the three-bedroom, 2,000-square-foot house Metz designed for Oliver and Suzanne Winston is stucco over concrete block, and the roof and back wall are weatherproofed with five-ply coal tar and felt. The soil, drawn back down over the roof after the house was built into the hillside, protects it from the weather and changes in temperature. The roof load is 285 pounds per square foot, because it must withstand not only a 15-inch layer of sod but also heavy snow and rain. A parapet of vertical Douglas fir quartersawn boards wraps around the house. From the road, only the V-shaped top of a light well and the chimney are seen. Of the sod roof, the owners say, "It's not a care; we don't even mow it."

Rough-sawn 6-by-10-inch yellow pine beams support the roof. Although the rear wall is dug into the hill and has no windows, the house is always bright. A splendid view of the mountains is seen from major rooms through the south wall of glass, which also acts as a passive solar collector. Deep overhangs keep the sun out in summer, and allow it in when it is desired in the fall, winter, and spring. A light well over the dining area admits not only sunlight but also moonbeams, which form changing shafts of light. "This is the only place we hear the patter of rain or the winds of a winter storm," says the owner. Two entries, spanned by a hall that runs the length of the house, give excellent ventilation. The garage and mud room are angled off the main structure (see plan). The outdoor terrace includes a little pool "for dunking."

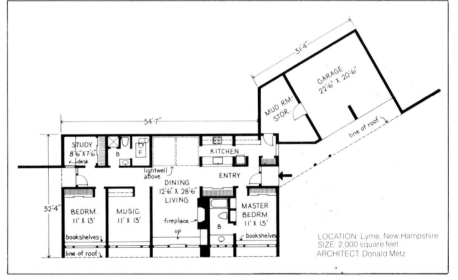

LOCATION: Lyme, New Hampshire
SIZE: 2,000 square feet
ARCHITECT: Donald Metz

Sod roof, above and left, where black-eyed Susans and Queen Anne's lace grow wild from summer to summer, helps protect the house from New Hampshire weather. From the road, only the V-shaped light well and the chimney can be seen.

All major rooms (see plan above and photos opposite) have south-facing walls of glass that let the sun in and permit wonderful views of the hillside into which the house has been built.

Underground houses

Snug in the earth, its face to the sun

Beneath its roof of earth and vegetation, a partly buried house in New Hampshire presents its face to the sun just as plants do.

In the living room: a stove for warmth.

Architect Donald Metz calls the passive solar home he designed for himself "a heliotropic house, presenting its face to the sun as a plant would." The second earth-covered structure that Mr. Metz has designed (see preceding pages), the rest of the house is almost entirely underground. The architect says this house is an "attempt to further define a terratectural vocabulary responsive to extreme loading conditions and heliotropic principles." His solution combines curvilinear forms and irregular framing systems in masonry and heavy timber. Large glazed areas on the southern exposure act as passive solar collectors, while bermed east and west walls and totally buried north walls expose a limited profile to the more severe elements. Overhangs, fin walls, and wing walls serve to limit wind-induced radiation while providing summer shade and reflected winter light. A wood- and/or oil-fired central heating unit delivers warm air via a double floor/plenum, warming the tiled floors as the air circulates to perimeter registers. A "heat bank" is established at the same time in the tons of concrete through which the warm air travels, resulting in a uniform schedule of heat distribution. Basement-level wood storage puts a full season's fuel (8 cords) under cover, humidifying the house as the wood dries throughout the winter.

From the north side, the Metz house is visible only as a mound of earth with steps leading down into the ground to the front door. To build the house, Mr. Metz dug into the side of the New Hampshire hill, peeling back the top layer of earth, then restoring it when the construction was completed. Now 8 inches of soil and abundant vegetation cover the roof. In contrast to all this earth-snugness, on the south, opposite, the house is glass-walled and open. Dramatic wing walls on either side of the glazed areas prevent winds from pulling away heat as they sweep around the aboveground parts of the house. On the partially earth-bermed east and west walls there are also windows, and these exposures have finlike projections between the glazed areas to reduce heat loss in the same way (see plan). Graceful contours are as much a part of the interior plan of the house as they are of the exterior.

On the south exposure, right, both the main living room and the lower level have glass walls. Chimneys on the roof serve the kitchen exhaust and two wood stoves, one each in the living and dining rooms. Built-in banquette seating, top, follows the curve of the living room wall. Windows on two sides of the dining room, above, pull in light and solar warmth. Parallel ceiling timbers, below, contrast with the curved walls. Brick floors, like the masonry walls, serve as thermal mass.

ROSS CHAPPLE

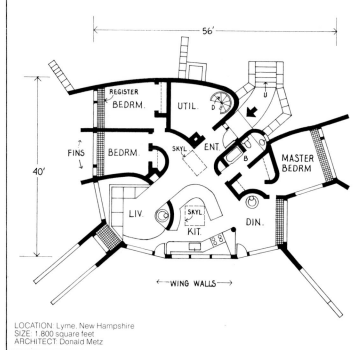

LOCATION: Lyme, New Hampshire
SIZE: 1,800 square feet
ARCHITECT: Donald Metz

The kitchen, above and opposite below, is the central gathering place in the house. Open to it are the dining room and the living room. The sweeping contour of the kitchen counter continues the curvilinear forms of the house. Just above it: one of two skylights.

Planning ahead for solar

A house ready for sun power

With the proper geometry and siting, this house was intentionally designed for easy conversion to an active system.

For his family's new home in Santa Barbara, Paul Gray decided to design a house that would be all the things the family wanted — light and open, social and private — and convertible from conventional to solar heat whenever they decide to make the change. Paul Gray is one of the growing number of architects who are convinced that solar energy is the way of the future. At the time he was building (1975), however, he saw some drawbacks. "The current high cost of using the sun's energy makes it too expensive for many people to consider. In a few years, I am sure there will be less expensive and more efficient systems available which will also be more aesthetically appealing." By providing the right geometry and siting, the handsome redwood house of shed-roofed elements that Mr. Gray designed can take the addition of a solar heat system with ease. The pitched roofs are metal, and solar panels, when added, will not detract from the good-looking contemporary design.

The expansive 3,900-square-foot house is a one-level design with different wings for different activities and rooms that look outdoors almost everywhere. The house was oriented to the southwest for maximum natural light and only a few trees cast their shadows on the walls. Throughout there are floor-to-ceiling windows and eight skylights. On the south side, big glass expanses are recessed to keep out the California sun in summer but admit it in winter, when the angle of the rays changes. The house is well insulated. Redwood tongue-and-groove vertical siding sheathes it, and inside there are 5½-inch-thick plaster walls. The four roofs that will receive collectors are pitched at 35 degrees. Areas outside have been designated as future solar energy storage zones. When the solar energy collection system is in place, the present forced-air system will become a backup unit.   [Continued]

DAVID MASSEY

The plan for the Gray house was decided upon after many drawings and several models — final model, right. Says Mr. Gray, "Family life is a mixture of interaction and privacy. The plan [next pages] reflects this: formal, informal, and private wings joined by hallways."

Pitched metal roofs, three views, above, will hold collectors. Now they provide fire protection in the dry southern California climate. Library roof, top, slants toward the south. Glass is everywhere: sliding glass doors for easy outdoor access, above center, round skylights on flat roof areas, bottom, bring in sunlight.

The house sits on three acres, with different wings for different activities. Model, opposite, shows library isolated at left; family areas beyond the entry; bedrooms, zoned for children and adults, to the right.

CHARLES WHITE

Swimming pool is dark brown to reflect the sun's heat.

Library, left of entry, is filled with natural light.

The house that architect Paul Gray designed for his family will someday call upon the sun for most of its energy, but even at this point it is attuned to nature. Large expanses of glass invite nature in at every glance: round skylights, big windows, sliding glass doors that give easy outdoor access. Metal roofs, where the collectors will be placed, also provide fire protection in the dry southern California climate. The house is sheathed in resawn redwood and sealed with a semitransparent stain. Silicon-sand concrete forms the paving outside, and a border of water-rounded rocks surrounds the house. Inside, each family activity has its own special zone. On the left of the entrance is the traffic-free living room/library. Straight ahead are the dining room, galley kitchen, and family room. The bedrooms are isolated on the north side. There are two bedrooms for three sons, one room for the daughter, and a playroom. A private suite for the parents occupies a dead-end corner. Hallways are used for displaying contemporary art and are covered in a practical low-pile carpeting that hides nail marks and also absorbs sound. Floors are 1-inch squares of wood parquet coated with urethane.

Balcony in library is semiprivate work space for Mr. Gray.

Water-rounded rock outlines and underscores the house.

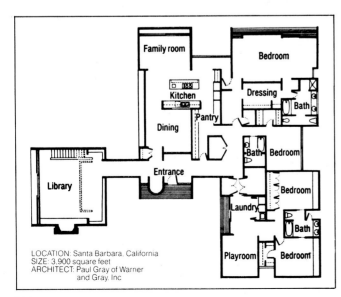

LOCATION: Santa Barbara, California
SIZE: 3,900 square feet
ARCHITECT: Paul Gray of Warner and Gray, Inc

Dining room, entry alcove, both have round skylights.

Master bedroom, in a private corner, overlooks the pool.

Wall of glass opens kitchen, dining room, to patio.

Rock pool, alongside swimming pool, is link with nature.

In the kitchen, storage and work space are abundant.

Shed roofs, like over family room, allow high glass areas.

Conceived as a timeless, rural building.

Decks connect house with guest unit.

For the owner, a "secret" terrace.

Designed to keep heating needs down

Made with hand-hewn joists and beams from the past, a timeless house was planned so that only its core need be heated in winter.

With roof pitched 58 degrees to the south so that it can eventually carry solar collectors, this house, designed by Charles Moore and built for writer Simone Swan on a small piece of land with a view of Long Island Sound, is energy-conscious and life-giving in a way that pleases all the senses. As the house was being designed, Simone Swan and her son, Eric, were researching the applications of such energy-saving alternative technologies as solar heating and waste recycling. In this process, they decided that a "more severe, pared to the bone" house would be more appropriate than the "cozy, rather worldly," house that they saw in an original model. So Charles Moore and his collaborator, Mark Simon, developed a design that became uncompromisingly rural with economical, straightforward, carpenterlike finishes. A square, hipped-roof form became an elongated shape with roof pitched to eventually carry solar collectors.

Already, however, the house is very energy-conscious. Beyond ensuring optimum insulation, and double glazing of all windows and French doors, it was designed so that only a part of the house need be heated in winter. The rooms are arranged around a central chimney for warmth in winter, and circulation through the house is from one room to the next without any need of a hall. The stair wraps around the chimney, which divides the narrow high interior into a living room at one end, a kitchen with dining area at the other. This cooking/dining/reading room is the heart of the house. Overhead, there is a bedroom/bath for the owner, and a small office or study, and this compact complex is all that needs to be heated in winter, when company is less likely on Long Island. For guests, winter or summer, there is a separate structure, connected to the main house by broad decking. In this guest unit are two bedrooms and a bath (see plan) that also do not have to be heated except when in use. Large 1-foot-thick foam cushions were designed by the architects to serve as living room furniture in the summer, but also to stack up, sealing the two large openings between the cooking/dining area and the living area during the winter. By this means, the living room can be left unheated and the house remains well insulated, saving considerable energy and cost.[*Continued*]

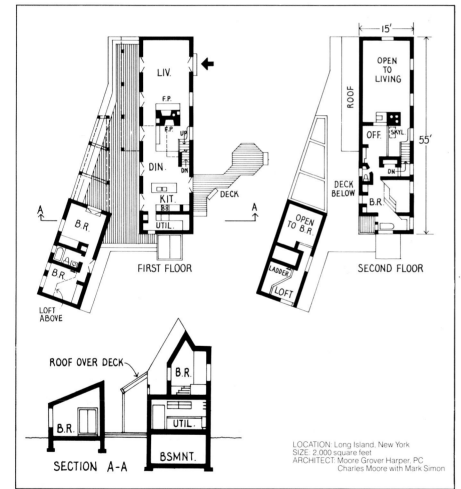

FIRST FLOOR

SECOND FLOOR

SECTION A-A

ROOF OVER DECK

LOCATION: Long Island, New York
SIZE: 2,000 square feet
ARCHITECT: Moore Grover Harper, PC
        Charles Moore with Mark Simon

Plans show how the Swan house is zoned to use as little heat as necessary. In the main house, bedroom and bath over the kitchen/dining area form one space for living that minimizes energy requirements. In the summer, this space is opened to the two-story-high living room at the other end of the house. Off by itself, a guest unit of two bedrooms and a bath. Section shows roof pitched 58 degrees.

In the handsome lower-level living spaces, the wood from an old barn is used to great advantage. These elements, from a stockpile of hand-hewn joists, flooring, and beams gleaned from an old farm building, are the legacy of the architect Louis Kahn, who died before he could begin to design Mrs. Swan's house. Before his death, however, he had encouraged her in her wish to buy and tear down an old farm building, the parts of which were ultimately arranged by Charles Moore and his collaborator, Mark Simon. Used as collar ties and trusses in the two-story living room, and on the lower dining and kitchen ceiling, they contribute to the rural farmhouse character of the house. In his design of the house, Charles Moore gave Mrs. Swan many of the things she had sought: "Bathing while looking at the trees, sitting in the winter sun protected from winds, a 'secret' tower terrace." One thing she didn't get was a clivus multrum, which was rejected as a not yet practical way to produce fertilizer for the vegetable garden. Mrs. Swan thinks this may have been a mistake. If so, it is a minor one in a house that not only expresses the owner's inner fantasies and dreams but meets her everyday needs as well.

The dining area with its own hearth.

An open kitchen with utensils on view.

The platform bed and claw-footed tub.

Collar ties and trusses in living room.

Mirrored skylights make most of light.

A double fireplace divides the living room, opposite, from the kitchen and its dining area on the other side. Shutters control sunlight from a wall of French doors; fan overhead provides a pleasant movement of air in the living room. Stair wraps around the central chimney, leading to the bedroom/bath and office overhead. In the bedroom, platform has cedar-lined drawers below; an old claw-footed bathtub is placed next to a window with a view of Long Island Sound.

ERNST BEADLE

Manufactured solar houses

Unique solar slab stores sun's heat

Generous insulated window areas and a patented solar slab for storage are the components of this prefabricated design.

Designed in a classic barn shape, this pine-sheathed two-story house has generous glass reaches on the south, east, and west sides to draw in the sun's energy. Once inside, it is distributed and used, or stored in a solar slab beneath the house (see section, right). In warm weather, the process is reversed, and the slab stores coolness, releasing it when the house becomes too warm. Made of concrete and gravel, the 4-foot-deep insulated slab also acts as the foundation of the prefabricated house by Green Mountain Homes. The prefabricated house and the solar slab, which has been patented, are the designs of James Kachadorian, an engineer by training. Built in Vermont in 1976, each has proved a resounding success according to the groups who are monitoring them, Dartmouth College's Thayer School of Engineering and the Central Vermont Public Service Corporation. During the harsh 1976–77 winter, before shutters were used in the house, only 406 gallons of oil ($249) were needed.

Mr. Kachadorian founded Green Mountain Homes in reaction to the soaring average costs of new houses in this country (currently $50,000). His company now manufactures prefabricated houses in the $14,850 to $53,000 range, excluding land. When the energy crisis hit, the designer-manufacturer developed the passive solar system now optional in all his houses. In addition to the windows, which serve as collectors, and the solar slab, for storage, there are other important energy-conservation features in the Green Mountain Homes. Two-inch-thick thermo-shutters are mounted inside to cover doors and windows; the walls, ceiling, and roof are well insulated. There is the option of a wood-burning stove or an energy-efficient heat-return fireplace for supplemental heat, plus a backup furnace. Green Mountain Homes also suggests landscaping to further conserve energy. Evergreens on the north side can act as a windbreak. Deciduous trees planted on the east, south, and west sides provide shade in warm months and allow the sun's rays to pass through in winter. It is estimated that the sun can provide half the heating of the house.

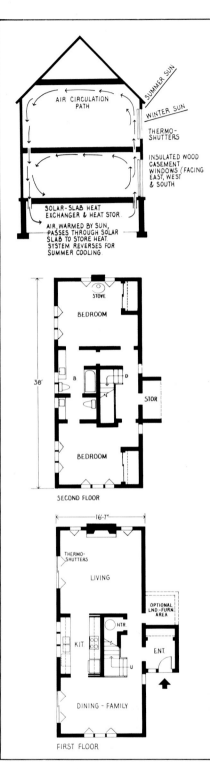

LOCATION: Vermont
SIZE: 1,264 square feet
DESIGNER: James Kachadorian

Once the sun's heat is brought into the house through the large glass expanses, it is mechanically distributed. The upstairs warms up first. When it reaches the desired temperature, set by a thermostat, the warm air is circulated to the downstairs by a blower mounted on the ceiling of the second floor. Then when the downstairs reaches its desired temperature (there is a second thermostat), the excess warm air is circulated to the solar slab beneath the house and stored for later use.

The barnlike design includes an extension (see plan above) that houses the foyer to reduce winter heat loss. A living room and dining/family room flank a kitchen and the separate entrance foyer on the first floor. Upstairs there are two bedrooms, two baths (a third bedroom can be added).

The solar system (slab, optional shutters, and extra windows) adds $2,500 to the cost of construction of the basic model—$26,900 if owner-built, $33,900 if contractor-constructed. For more information on this or other designs, send $1.50 to Green Mountain Homes, Royalton, Vermont 05068.

Manufactured solar houses

A factory-built solar house on Cape Cod

In 1974, Acorn Structures began developing a solar system for its manufactured houses. Here is the first one built; solar energy provided half the heat during its first year of occupancy.

Acorn Structures, a designer and manufacturer of factory-built houses in the northeast, has one of the first integrated active solar energy prefab housing design packages available. Working since 1974 on the development of a space heating and domestic hot water system for it prefabricated houses, the firm introduced a solar version of its four-bedroom North Cape model in 1976 that would meet the special requirements of energy conservation and solar heating. The first Acorn solar house is the one here, built as a retirement home for Mr. and Mrs. George Brickelmaier on Cape Cod in Massachusetts. The Brickelmaiers had lived in southern California and decided that when they moved to the colder northeast they would build a solar-heated house. They chose an Acorn house, modifying one of the firm's trim North Cape designs to meet their requirements, but including the new option of having solar panels fitted to the sloping roof, of their new house. The eight 4-by-20-foot flat-plate collectors, manufactured by Sunwave, mounted on the south-facing roof, circulate water to be warmed by the sun, then sent to storage in a tank in the basement. Enough energy to help heat the house for several days can be stored in the 2,000-gallon solar storage tank.

The building was designed and sited so that solar collectors would be housed on the southerly side, yet broad expanses of south-facing glass have been maintained. The overhangs shade the glass when the sun is high in the summer but allow the sun to help heat the living spaces in the winter. Heating-system return ducts distribute this sun-warmed air from the south side and from the design's high cathedral spaces to the rest of the house. Windows have double-insulating glass, and windows and doors are weather-stripped. There are few windows on the north side, and a dense growth of pine around the house screens it from the fierce Cape Cod winter wind. Acorn's standard construction specifies maximum insulation in the walls, the roof, and the floors. [Continued]

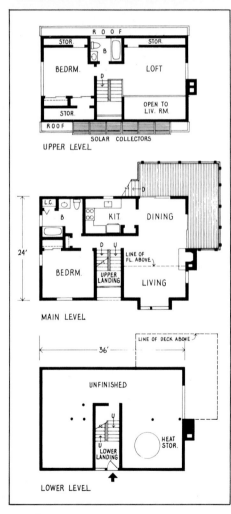

LOCATION: Cape Cod, Massachusetts
SIZE: 1,500 square feet
MANUFACTURER: Acorn Structures

Plans above, show the multilevel plan of the Brickelmaier house. Main level includes a living/dining room, kitchen, deck, and guest suite. The master bedroom is on the upper level, where a loft provides space for music, crafts.

STEVE ROSENTHAL

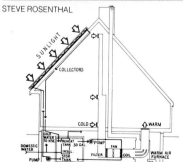

Solar collectors mounted on the south-facing roof, above, collect the sun's energy, which is then distributed throughout the house. Windows also draw in sunlight. A manufactured house, almost all parts of this structure arrive on a truck to be assembled by a local contractor. A side view, opposite top, shows the raised deck and rock garden, plus basement level, which opens directly on grade through a pair of sliding glass doors.

Although the initial cost of the solar heat system was substantial — it added $7,200 to the cost of the house—it has proved very efficient. It supplies about 45 percent of the space heating and 64 percent of the hot water needs, or 47 percent of the total heat and hot water needs in an average year. Last year a mere $154 was spent on heating their house. In addition, the owners receive a $200 solar tax credit each year for ten years under Massachusetts law. Since the initial development of the solar system for this design, Acorn Structures has added two Solar Capes and a solar garage to its line of houses. Plans for one of the new house designs are shown below.

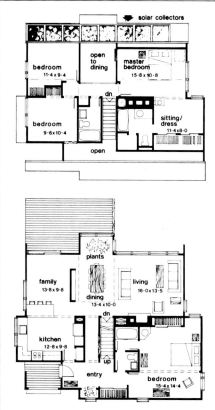

Like all Acorn houses, the Solar Capes (see plan of one above) are sold through a local contractor-builder. "When you buy one, Acorn sends a representative to supervise the construction." For additional details write to Acorn Structures, Box 250, Concord, Massachusetts 01742. The plan above is for Acorn's Solar Cape 1950. A slightly larger version, the Solar Cape 2300, is also available. Prices range from $75,000 for Model 1950 to $92,000 for Model 2300 with garage and connecting breezeway. Estimates include the solar system, which may be deleted at $7,900.

STEVE ROSENTHAL

Ceiling, windows, peak in bedroom.

Music loft overlooks living room below.

Stairs are spine of multi-level plan.

Electric storage heating
Designed to utilize sun, wood, and electricity

In a passive solar design, an energy-efficient wood stove plus electrical storage heating supplement the sun's energy to warm this Vermont house.

The pine-sheathed passive solar house nestles on its Vermont site.

There are many advantages to electric heating — its ease of installation, control, cleanliness, and safety. But cost is not usually one of them. This Vermont house capitalizes on the advantages, while minimizing the cost disadvantages through a relatively new electrical storage heating system that utilizes off-peak generating capacity to satisfy on-peak heating requirements. The energy storage is provided at the consumer end of the distribution network; heaters are charged only during control periods, usually late night, early morning hours, such as 11:00 P.M. to 7:00 A.M. During this eight-hour period, sufficient heat is placed into the unit's storage core to allow the heaters to maintain desirable room temperatures. Industrial designer Richard Penney specified the electric storage heating units (Permatherm-F by Siemens) in his second house, a passive solar design in southwestern Vermont. A two-story window on the south elevation acts as a passive collector, and a Defiant wood stove in the living room can also heat the 1,400-square-foot house.

The house itself is a combination of 17th-century and contemporary architectural detailing on the exterior and a synthesis of Shaker and contemporary planning on the interior. In designing the house, Mr. Penney gave a great deal of attention to conservation of energy without specific hardware, and its associated costs. "I built a house which costs no more than the average," he says, "but accomplished recognizable savings in the energy required."

Windows were kept to a minimum on the north and east elevations, while the large south window has the dual role of aesthetics and passive collection of solar heat. Windows in the two bedrooms are oriented to the west to capture the warmth of the sun toward the end of the day, plus light. Because of the house's location in southwestern Vermont, the sun angles are very low in the winter, giving long light and heat, and high during the summer when less heat is desirable. Also in the summer, an angled interior window in the two-story plan can be left open to effect natural convection with hot air rising and going out skylights in the north roof.

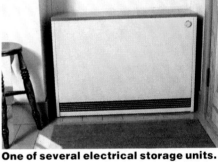
Angled window permits convection.

One of several electrical storage units.

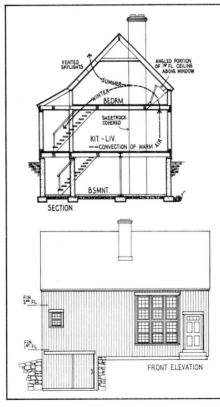

LOCATION: Southwestern Vermont
SIZE: 1,400 square feet
DESIGNER: Richard Penney

Historic concepts of how a house should be designed are reflected in the low-ceilinged spaces of the Penney house. "Rooms are as large as they need to be, but no larger." Plan shows one large open living space, above, and a master bedroom and bath on the lower level, a large combination bedroom and studio upstairs, plus a second bath.

Shaker influence is seen in the simple furnishings, opposite, their tenets of efficiency, which have beauty and serenity as by-products. Defiant wood stove can heat entire house; chimney runs up through the center core of the house and any reradiation of heat benefits surrounding living areas.

ERNST BEADLE

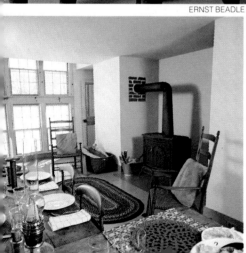

Retrofitting

In solar parlance, retrofitting initially meant adapting existing structures for solar heating systems; but as interest in passive as well as active solar energy technology has grown, retrofitting has come to include any remodeling with the sun in mind. And why not? The sun, which has no meters and sends no bills, shines on houses long standing as well as on those being newly built.

There are over 70 million houses in the United States today. The vast majority of these are easily adaptable to solar domestic hot water heating, at least, while a significant number could be redesigned for heating as well. Admittedly it is trickier to install the means for collecting and distributing solar heat to an existing house, but it has been estimated that at least 60 percent of the buildings in the country have the capacity for utilizing some of the sun's energy.

There are many ways to collect, store, and distribute solar heat in existing houses. A south-facing window will collect but not store. A brick floor or masonry wall that gets a great deal of sunshine can collect, store, and distribute — but offer no exacting controls: They simply absorb excess heat when the sun shines on them and radiate that heat after dark when surrounding air is cooler. Inventive combinations of such familiar building components as brick and glass may be all that are needed to accomplish small wonders. Complex solar heating systems capable of collecting, storing, and distributing heat when and where it is wanted can provide much of the energy needed for space heating and for domestic hot water. Those systems that involve sophisticated components and engineering are for the most talented and dedicated of do-it-yourselfers or are best left to expert designers and contractors.

In retrofitting, as in new construction, whatever the energy source — conventional fuels or the sun — preventing heat loss and reducing energy requirements by eliminating unnecessary use come first. Too little insulation, windows with only single glazing, joints where outside air can infiltrate — these cause tremendous amounts of heat loss. Solving those problems can cut heating bills more, and for less cash outlay, than more dramatic measures requiring extensive structural changes. For example, during each heating season, a good insulating shutter with a tight seal around it should save about 40,000 to 75,000 BTUs per square foot — even more in a severe climate, say, of 8,000 degree-days — and that is about the same amount that various types of collectors in passive systems will collect. Only after heat loss is minimized and heat-conserving measures are adopted is it time to consider how solar energy can help heat rooms or domestic hot water or both. Then there are many ways to begin retrofitting.

Collectors for a solar heating system, or domestic hot water supply, at least, can be installed on the roof, on a wall, on the ground close to the house or somewhat away from it. The leeway makes it possible to take advantage of a sunnier site, perhaps a less obtrusive one or a place where the desired tilt for the collector is easier to achieve. The roof of a garage, or another utility building, could be used for solar collectors, and, if necessary, part of the interior could house a rock bin or other heat storage. Whenever possible, however, the storage unit should be in the building to be heated to prevent excessive loss of heat in distribution.

With the addition of a greenhouse, the whole unit could serve as a solar collector by adding it on a sunny part of the house. Trapped, sun-warmed air can be directed into the house by dampers and registers. Attached to any side of the house, a glassed-in porch could also help save fuel, somewhat like a giant storm window in effect, but with much more potential. Glass-walled and added to the south, the porch could let sun-heated air enter the house through existing windows. On any side, the porch would cut down on heat loss through windows and doors and from joints on that part of the house. When used as an entrance, it would work the way a vestibule does, keeping cold air out of the rest of the house.

Certainly retrofitting should be considered in any plan to add a wing to an existing house. Starting with proper orientation, a complete solar heating system could be installed as if in a new house.

But even less ambitious projects can be part of a retrofit program. For example, adding a window on the south side of a house is a much favored way to gain solar energy. If a window is undesirable, perhaps because of a dull view, a road nearby, or too-close neighbors, a lean-to that has air heating collectors and a well-insulated container for rocks (which store solar heat for nighttime use) could be a possibility. A fan blows air from the house through the warm rocks and back into the room needing heat.

An exposed masonry wall to the south can also serve as an effective solar collector. A concrete, brick, or stone wall, which naturally absorbs the sun's heat, can be converted into a combined collector and storage unit to help warm the adjoining interior space and also hold excess heat, releasing it at night when the room begins to cool. To make it a better solar collector, the wall should be painted a dark color on its exterior, covered with glass or plastic, leaving a little space between wall and glass to trap heat gained. With openings cut toward the top and bottom, controlled by dampers, warm air heated by the sun will rise in the space between the wall and glass and flow into the rooms while cooler air is drawn in at floor level. An insulating cover to go over the glass at night could double the savings in fuel. The simplest version, one that will reduce fuel use somewhat, would be just the masonry wall with dark coating and glass but no openings or insulating cover.

With the growth of interest in solar energy for residential use, there has been a parallel growth in workshops, courses, and publications designed to further solar knowhow. Total Environmental Action, Inc., is a Harrisville, New Hampshire– based firm of architects and engineers concerned with conservation and solar energy. TEA conducts one-day courses on retrofitting several times a year. In the course, which is open to the public for a small fee, instructor Dan Scully makes the following points in answer to frequently asked questions:

What is the most direct way to use solar energy? Add a south-facing window. There is just as much energy available to a window as to a complex solar collector. Over an entire heating season, a south-facing window gains more heat than it loses.

What if a house doesn't face due south? There's sufficient energy available in other ranges to provide real benefits. For a location at 40 degrees latitude, for example, a window that is about 25 degrees to the east or west of due south would receive approximately 90 percent of the radiation striking a south-facing window. In planning any solar energy project it is important to know where the sun is coming from and when it can get in and when it can't. The nearest weather station has data about its area.

Is a solar heating system just for domestic water worthwhile? Generally, yes. A water heater is the second largest user of energy in most houses — water heating is needed twelve months of the year, not part of the year as space heating is. Installing a solar heating system for domestic hot water is a project that many homeowners can manage. It requires fewer collectors and less money than a system designed to help heat rooms.

What should the tilt be for roof collectors? The rule of thumb is latitude plus 10 degrees for collectors for a space heating system and just latitude for collectors for a domestic hot water system. But some people are overly concerned about achieving the ideal tilt; there is a range of angles within which very acceptable amounts of energy can be collected. Also, collectors don't have to go on a roof; they can be completely separate from the house itself. There are all kinds of trade-offs to consider — in design as well as in the energy you get.

On the following pages we show two retrofits: The first is a sophisticated passive solar remodeling; the second is the addition of a new wing, fitted with active solar collectors, to an 1805 house.

Retrofitting
Insulation, innovation, help in conservation

An early 1960s house gains more glass, more living space, in a remodeling designed to cut fuel consumption.

Among the few exterior changes, a deeper overhang to shade the deck.

Remodeled for energy conservation and year-round use in 1974, this one-time vacation retreat on 17 acres in Chester, Connecticut, now has more glass, more living space, and more livability — yet uses less oil than ever before. The remodeling architect, Donald Watson (author of *Designing and Building a Solar House,* Garden Way Publishing, Charlotte, Vermont), almost doubled the total living space but changed its volumes to reflect post-fuel-crunch energy-consciousness. Major rooms — a huge multipurpose living area and the master bedroom — were located on the upper level because it commands a marvelous view of the woods and a river beyond. An existing wall of glass — with only single glazing — brought in the view and in winter allowed the cold to enter, too. The ceiling reached high, its exposed structural planking was attractive, its insulation meager.

The owner wanted the house made more comfortable for year-round use, with additional living space and less fuel consumption. To do this, the architect lowered the ceiling, introduced pleasant curved forms and a banquette. A dramatic light well was added along one side. Bounded by glass on the lower level, the shaft reaches up from the slab foundation to the second floor and beyond — to a 20-foot-long and 4-foot-wide curved skylight. During cold sunless hours or in too-hot weather, a translucent insulating panel can be moved across the upper shaft, just below the skylight. In cool weather, when sun is available and its warmth wanted, this panel as well as insulating panels elsewhere can be pushed aside. In the winter, the sun enters the lower window wall which is shaded by trees in summer. It strikes masonry flooring which absorbs and stores solar heat, distributing the excess after the sun has gone down. To provide extra warmth without requiring more fuel oil, a wood stove has taken over the downstairs hearth. A Jotul model, it burns wood more efficiently than the fireplace did. Dead wood comes from the property — for free. Before remodeling, from September 1973 to September 1974, 1,020 gallons of oil were used for the heating system. The year after remodeling, 750 gallons were used, despite the fact that more living space was being heated.

Insulating panels were added.

Insulating panels control light and heat from the sun: Shutters can be pulled across glass doors on lower floor, above and opposite above left; a movable translucent panel can close off the skylight over the two-story well, opposite. This panel, made by Kalwall, has two sheets of fiberglass held slightly apart by aluminum framing; within is mineral wool insulation.

The light well, opposite, has a "roof monitor" system that includes an air return high in the shaft to recirculate warmed air in winter, and a ventilating fan to help cool the house in summer. Insulating glass was installed in all existing windows, and Thermopane was used whenever new glass was decreed.

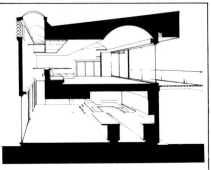

Drawing, by permission: © Donald Watson: *Designing and Building a Solar House,* 1977.

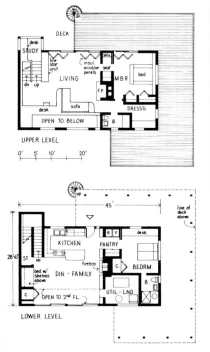

LOCATION: Chester, Connecticut
SIZE: 2,120 square feet
ARCHITECT: Donald Watson

Retrofitting
1805 house gets new wing and solar heat

Two-story glass-walled sunroom addition with collectors on its roof makes up hybrid system in Baltimore renovation.

Solar collectors on the new wing.

Inside: a new and efficient kitchen.

Handmade mantel in the restored living room was found in the house.

Part of Baltimore's "house for a dollar" homesteading program, this house combines serious restoration of its early-19th-century architecture with a late-20th-century solar energy heating system. The owner, general contractor Anne Dorrett, has added to her 1805 house a wing that includes a two-story sunroom with a south-facing glass wall that serves as a passive solar collector and greenhouse. On the new wing's roof, flat-plate solar collectors have been installed to give the newly renovated house an active heat-pump-assisted solar system for both space heating and domestic hot water. In the new wing, a trim efficient kitchen is housed on the first floor along with the two-story-high sunroom; upstairs there is a luxurious compartmented bath/dressing/laundry suite off the curved sunroom balcony (see plans, right). Ms. Dorrett removed a ramshackle back addition from the original three-story house to make way for the new solar-powered wing.

The Dorrett house is part of the Old Otterbein Homestead Area of Baltimore, one of the first cities to include homesteading in its housing strategy. The homesteading program in Baltimore makes available for one dollar a vacant deteriorated house that the city has acquired, usually by tax default. Homesteaders are assisted financially by low-interest loans and trained resource staff. The homesteader must move into the house within six months, and must remain in residence for another year and a half. At that point, a final inspection is made to see that building codes and architectural guidelines have been met, and a deed is presented. Only from then on are taxes levied. Owners like Ms. Dorrett and her neighbors acted with the city and planning consultants Land Design/Research to establish standards and guidelines for the area, including the application of solar energy technology. Because of Otterbein architectural guidelines for front façades and roof lines, solar collection devices can only appear on rear or nonpublic sides of housing units, or on new additions in rear yards as was done in the Dorrett house.

A luxurious bath, also in new wing.

The new wing of the Dorrett house includes a two-story sunroom, opposite, with a south-facing glass wall that acts as a passive solar collector. It is topped by a roof equipped with solar collectors that serve the active side of the system.

The plan, right, shows how the renovated building consists of two distinct parts: the original 1805 structure with its traditional, restored living room, dining room, bedroom, and study; the new wing with its modern kitchen and bath, the passive/active hybrid solar system.

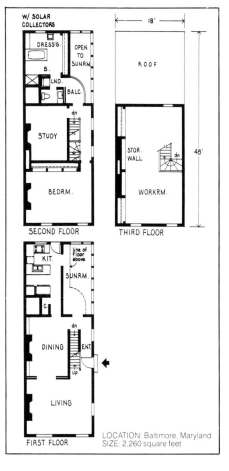

SECOND FLOOR

THIRD FLOOR

FIRST FLOOR

LOCATION: Baltimore, Maryland
SIZE: 2,260 square feet

ROBERT PERRON

132

3 projects show new regional aesthetic

"Stack effect" natural ventilation, rock-bed cooling, solar space heating water wall, and exterior "environmental graphics" combine in a sophisticated solar design for southern California.

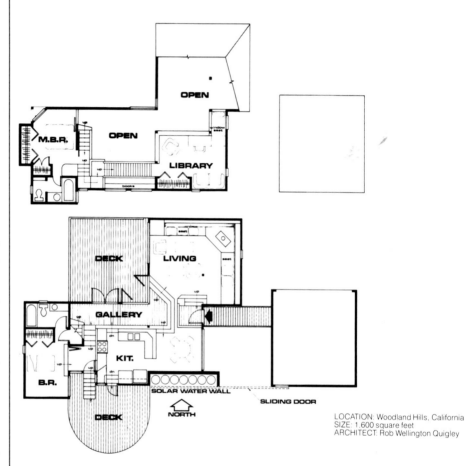

LOCATION: Woodland Hills, California
SIZE: 1,600 square feet
ARCHITECT: Rob Wellington Quigley

In a growing number of architectural offices across the country, there are design projects on drawing boards that reveal a new awareness among architects and designers of the importance of energy-conscious design and the impact integrated solar systems will have on the aesthetics of architecture. One such office is in San Diego, where architect Rob Wellington Quigley speaks of the conflict between those architects who feel that "beauty is what we're used to" and those who feel that "what we're used to is irresponsible design." According to this architect, "a new regional aesthetic will eventually emerge as designers break free of preconceptions, engineers define more precisely the passive vocabulary, and the public becomes more educated." The three projects on these and the following two pages are part of that process. They show some of the new architectural concepts and directions the architect is speaking about. All of these will have been built by the time of this book's publication; a Quigley-designed solar house finished in time to be included may be seen on pages 68 through 71.

The first house, opposite, designed for a young couple with one child, is now under construction in southern California, where the climate is one of hot days and cool evenings. The modest 1,600-square-foot structure uses standard 2-by-4-inch stud framing and catalogue parts throughout to meet a tight budget. The house is organized around a 10-by-10-by-25-foot-high belvedere tower, which is pierced by a linear gallery (see plan, right). The gallery begins at the garage as the entry bridge, passes under a window seat and through the front doors to reveal the dining room, below at the left; living room on the right; and library, above. The gallery then continues through the base of the belvedere, past the kitchen and living deck to the two bedrooms and baths stacked beyond.

The open space organized around the tower (see section, opposite) allows the house to act as a chimney, guiding the rising hot air to the belvedere, venting it through large turbans at the ceiling. During periods that are too hot or cold to allow this natural air flow, a large damper, like a kinetic sculpture in the throat of the tower, is used to close off the unneeded belvedere volume, reducing the area to be cooled or heated.

The house has three separate natural energy mechanical systems. Solar space heating is provided by a water wall with a standard gas-fired forced-air heater backup. The water wall is an insulated box, glazed on the south side, which contains standing columns of water to store the sun's heat. At night, an insulated barn door is closed over the glazing to prevent heat loss. The second system provides natural cooling. A large rock bed is contained in the crawl space under the child's bedroom. It is cooled by circulating cold late night air each evening with a small fan. On days too hot for the house's "stack effect" natural ventilation, the windows and damper are closed and the house air is simply routed through the cold rock bed and distributed through the same duct system used for heating. The third system heats the domestic hot water and employs an "off-the-shelf" active system by a local manufacturer. The single solar collector needed by the system is located on the belvedere and uses the sunshade below to gain reflected radiation.

Wood frame windows are not only devices to frame selected views but are also solar collectors. They will be carefully shaded by landscaping on the hot west side and controlled by sunshades on the south, opposite above. The canvas shades wind around 16mm movie projector sprockets at the corners of the windows and are adjustable for fine tuning by the occupants. They have been calculated to allow only the warming winter rays to penetrate the house.

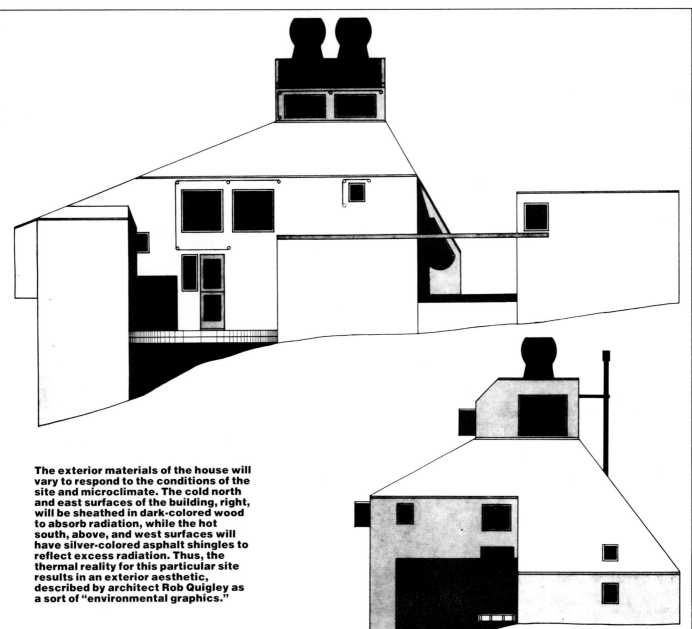

The exterior materials of the house will vary to respond to the conditions of the site and microclimate. The cold north and east surfaces of the building, right, will be sheathed in dark-colored wood to absorb radiation, while the hot south, above, and west surfaces will have silver-colored asphalt shingles to reflect excess radiation. Thus, the thermal reality for this particular site results in an exterior aesthetic, described by architect Rob Quigley as a sort of "environmental graphics."

ROB WELLINGTON QUIGLEY

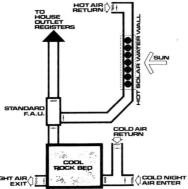

The solar space heating water wall, left, works with a standard gas-fired forced-air heater. Return air is routed into the south-facing 8-by-12-foot solar box to be preheated before it reaches the furnace. The air is moved by the fan inside the backup furnace. The furnace itself ignites only if air from the solar box is not warm enough.

A fan on a timber blows cold nighttime air through the rock bed, left, during summer and winter hot spells. With windows and damper closed, house air is simply routed through the cold rock bed and distributed through the duct system for cooling.

Designed for an area with Spanish Mediterranean design restrictions, glass-covered heat-lag walls with the look of windows provide space heating for a passive solar house.

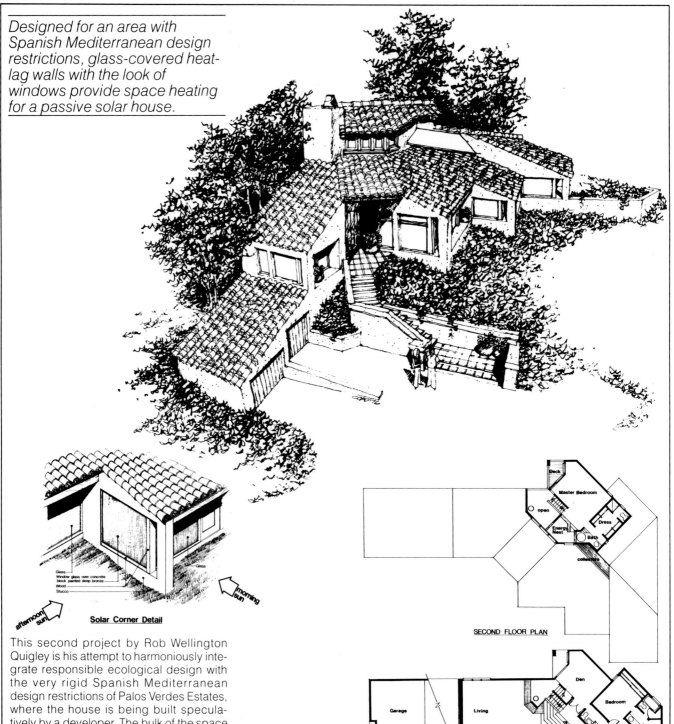

Solar Corner Detail

Glass
Window glass over concrete block painted deep bronze
Wood
Stucco
Glass
morning sun
afternoon sun

SECOND FLOOR PLAN

Deck
Master Bedroom
open
Energy Nest
Dress
Bath
collectors

Garage
Living
Den
Bedroom
Bedroom
Dining
Kitchen
Breakfast
Family Room

FIRST FLOOR PLAN
0 5 10 20

This second project by Rob Wellington Quigley is his attempt to harmoniously integrate responsible ecological design with the very rigid Spanish Mediterranean design restrictions of Palos Verdes Estates, where the house is being built speculatively by a developer. The bulk of the space heating will be accomplished passively by using the house itself as a solar collector through what Quigley calls his "energy sawtooth" concept. The "sawtooth" architecturally integrates calculated overhangs, kinetic insulation, floor-slab heat storage, and heat-lag walls. The majority of the glass in the house faces southeast to take advantage of the warming morning sun. The fireplace will become a viable heating source by introducing an exterior combustion air pipe and exposing the two-story flue on the interior. Placed on the interior of the structure to avoid heat loss through exterior walls, it is surrounded by solid masonry to increase the thermal mass of the house.

The solar corner detail, above left, shows how some of the glazing incorporated in the house's passive solar design actually covers concrete walls, painted deep bronze, for a Trombe-wall effect. The hot afternoon sun will be captured by these masonry heat-lag walls and saved for nighttime reradiation. All windows will be double glazed and have insulated shutters to decrease nighttime heat losses. An "off-the-shelf" active solar system will provide domestic hot water. It will require only about 50 square feet of flat-plate collectors, tucked into the roof forms like a skylight.

LOCATION: Palos Verdes, California
SIZE: 3,000 square feet
ARCHITECT: Rob Wellington Quigley

Climatic building system plugs solar responsive nodes into a nonresponsive production core to make possible solar houses built within tract-housing constraints.

Exploring the possibilities of climatic design for developers within the market constraints of detached dwellings on suburban lots, as well as technical constraints of existing tract-house construction techniques, Rob Quigley designed this "low-cost" production building system that uses traditional light frame and stucco construction. A repetitive core containing the plumbing, garage, and sleeping space is oriented to the street. To this "nonresponsive" core are added the "responsive" living space nodes. These nodes twist and turn to orient to the sun, and avoid shading the neighboring house. The nodes also take on various personalities to give the house a feeling of individual identity.

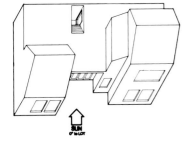

When the sun is at right angles to the street, the problem is much simpler, as is shown in the sketch above. An "energy sawtooth" variation would also be possible with the sun at +45 degrees to the street, as it is in the Point Loma Palms scheme, right.

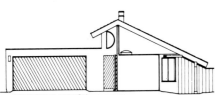

SUBURBAN RANCH (45° SUN)

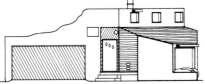

MISSION REVIVAL (45° SUN)

A "Suburban Ranch" and a "Mission Revival" variation on architect Rob Quigley's building system has been completed for $25 a square foot. Adherence to sound passive design, such as a windowless north wall, gave innovative developer Bill Houlihan of San Diego a bonus in the effective zero side-yard setback.

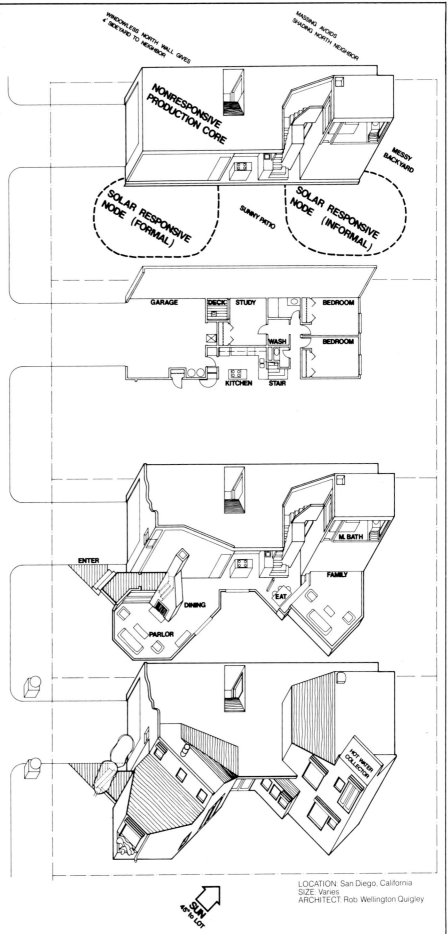

WINDOWLESS NORTH WALL GIVES 4' SIDEYARD TO NEIGHBOR

MASSING AVOIDS SHADING NORTH NEIGHBOR

NONRESPONSIVE PRODUCTION CORE

MESSY BACKYARD

SOLAR RESPONSIVE NODE (FORMAL)

SUNNY PATIO

SOLAR RESPONSIVE NODE (INFORMAL)

GARAGE · DECK · STUDY · BEDROOM
WASH · BEDROOM
KITCHEN · STAIR

ENTER · M. BATH · FAMILY · EAT · DINING · PARLOR

HOT WATER COLLECTOR

SUN 45° to LOT

LOCATION: San Diego, California
SIZE: Varies
ARCHITECT: Rob Wellington Quigley

Solar house plans to order by mail

Complete plans and materials lists can be ordered for the following five houses: three active solar houses, one passive solar design, and one underground house with an active solar system. Plans for these houses are available through House & Garden at $75.00 each. Five sets for one house cost $105.00, and additional sets for the same house ordered at the same time are $15.00 each. One set provides what a builder needs to begin estimates and start construction, but you will probably need extra blueprints as well, unless you are ordering them only to study, to help you to choose a site or to see if the plans you like will work on property you already own. If you are ordering in anticipation of building immediately, you will want a set to retain for your own use, one for the builder-contractor, one for the mortgagee, one for the local building department, and perhaps one for an architect or solar engineer to help you adjust these plans to your particular situation. When selecting a plan, keep in mind how important orientation to the sun is in the success of a solar house. Plans cannot be sent on approval and they are not returnable.

Ordering instructions.

Please order carefully. Be sure to include the house number of the plan you want to order. Also indicate how you want plans mailed. Unless you send air mail or special delivery postage, allow at least three weeks for delivery. Be sure to include your correct address, the number of sets of plans you want, and the price of the quantity of plans you decide to order: one set for one house, $75.00; five sets for one house, $105.00; additional sets for same house, each $15.00. Add the following costs for postage to your check: parcel post, $2.00; air mail or special delivery (one set), $3.00; overseas air mail (one set), $5.00; air mail or special delivery (more than one set), $5.00; and overseas air mail (more than one set), $10.00. Mail to House & Garden, Dept. SHP-1, P.O. Box 1910, Grand Central Station, New York, New York 10017.

RENDERINGS: LEWIS BRYDEN

SECOND FLOOR

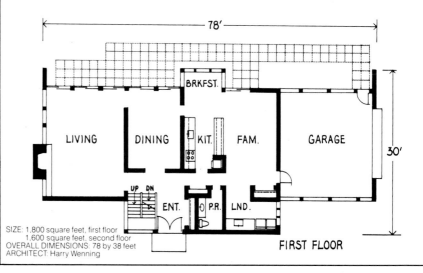

SIZE: 1,800 square feet, first floor
1,600 square feet, second floor
OVERALL DIMENSIONS: 78 by 38 feet
ARCHITECT: Harry Wenning

FIRST FLOOR

Flat-plate collectors provide solar heat

Behind a rustic contemporary shingle and stone façade, a generous sloping roof holds the collector array for a large two-story family house.

The shingle and stone façade of this handsome two-story contemporary structure gives no sign of the active solar heating system that is designed to provide a significant part of the energy for the house's space heating and domestic hot water needs. But on the back, south-facing elevation a generous sloping roof holds the array of flat-plate collectors designed to collect the energy of the sun. From the roof, heat is transferred by water through copper tubing to a 4,000-gallon storage tank under the garage. In the event of cold, sunless days, two electric heat pumps are provided in the plan as a backup system.

The house, designed by architect Harry Wenning, is large: 1,800 square feet on the first floor, 1,600 square feet on the second floor, plus a generous basement for family recreation and workshop space. Thanks to the angle of the roof, calculated to accept solar collectors, there is also a space bonus in the attic, reached by a disappearing stair in the upstairs hall. Entry to the house is through a formal entry near the glass-enclosed stairway, or via a more everyday route from garage through the family room to kitchen or front hall. Across the rear of the house, sliding glass doors open every lower-level room to a house-wide terrace. These glass walls in the living room, dining room, and family room allow entry of the sun's rays in winter, while a cantilevered screen protects the rooms from summer sun. The kitchen has its own sun-warmed area, a glassed-in dinette that projects into the terrace area, somewhat dividing the outdoor living area into formal and informal zones. By contrast, windows are limited on the colder, north-facing front of the house. Instead, walls of stone and high R-value cedar shingles keep out cold.

Upstairs there are four bedrooms, three baths, and two decks. The master bedroom is a self-contained suite, with its own deck, dressing room, bath, and walk-in closet. On the south, two equal-sized bedrooms have windows recessed in the collector array and share a bath. On the north, a fourth bedroom with shower bath and its own deck would make a super self-contained suite for guests.

Because this is a large house, the collector area for solar heat has to be equally large. Architect Harry Wenning provides 1,200 square feet of collector array along the south-facing rear of the house. The slope of the roof continues to the ground at each side of the 78-foot-wide house, partially screening outdoor living areas that range along the back of the house. Beneath the collectors, sliding glass doors open rooms to the warming low-angled rays of the sun in winter. A cantilevered roof, extending on each side of the dinette bay projection, provides protection from the higher-angled rays of the summer sun.

Solar house plan No. 2

Central atrium captures sunlight

Overhead, Skylids form an "instant roof" to keep warm air in on cool nights; below, paving retains and radiates the heat of the sun to surrounding spaces.

The heart of this house, and of its fuel-conservation system, is a sun-oriented atrium that draws solar heat through a glass roof and retains and radiates it through a paved floor. Designed by architect Alfredo De Vido, the passive solar house has conventional plumbing and heating, but uses every possible means, especially the sun, to conserve fuel. Among its energy-conserving attributes: a compact shape with minimal exterior surfaces exposed to cold weather; front and back door wind screens plus vestibules to minimize heat loss; interior insulating shutters for all windows plus an exterior skin that is variously weatherproofed.

Solar heat coming through the south-facing glass-roofed atrium warms surrounding spaces. Three interior sliding glass window walls open to the entry, family and living rooms. Doors to these rooms can be closed when the atrium cools, and for winter nights automatic louvers — Skylids from Zomeworks — form a protective "instant roof." This same core space cools the house in summer by letting rising warm air out through an operable vent at the top, thereby pulling cool air in through the sides of the house (see sections, opposite). The upper section shows how seasonal sun angles are controlled and exploited. Overhangs are calculated to admit winter-angled sun but to block the summer sun's rays. The lower section shows the second-floor winter room, located to collect heat from the upper reaches of the living room plus south roof glazing that could make this a delightful studio space. A secondary glass roof covers a greenhouse (see plan, right). Among the various weatherproofing techniques are double glazing, caulked wall joints, heavy insulation. The freestanding fireplace is of the heat-generating type, and its flue is exposed to also radiate heat. The chimney housing on the exterior includes a large exhaust fan to supplement ventilation incorporated in the glass roof.

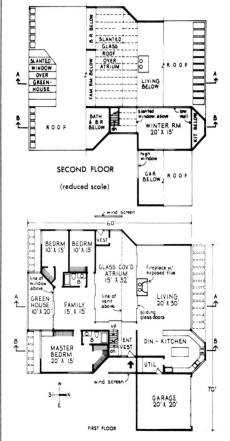

SECOND FLOOR
(reduced scale)

FIRST FLOOR

SIZE: 2,420 square feet, first floor
340 square feet, second floor
OVERALL DIMENSIONS: 60 by 70 feet
ARCHITECT: Alfredo De Vido

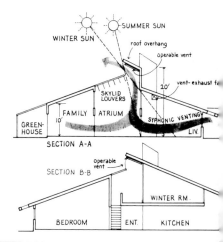

RENDERINGS: LEWIS BRYDEN

The sun-gathering atrium not only aids in energy conservation, but adds marvelous design drama to both the exterior and interior of the passive solar house (see drawings, opposite). Interior glass walls open and close as temperatures dictate, but always provide a visual flow of space through living/atrium/family room areas. Paving on the floor is not only good for plants, but stores and radiates the collected heat of the sun. To order this plan, write House & Garden, *Dept. SHP–1, P.O. Box 1910, Grand Central Station,* New York, New York 10017, and refer to Solar House No. 2. A second version of this plan, with two more bedrooms and a bath above the garage, opening off the winter room, can be ordered as Solar House No. 2A.

SECTION A-A

SECTION B-B

140

Solar house plan No. 3

Skylids, collectors, trap the sun's heat

Utilizing readily available components, a hybrid solar house design has a greenhouse to maximize the benefits of living with the sun.

This handsome design by architect Alfredo De Vido stands tall to reach for the sun, natural cooling, and lighting. Four collector modules top the south roof, opposite below, to make up the active part of the solar heating system. Underneath the flat-plate collector array, heat-trap spaces on the same southern exposure act as passive collectors. In one of those spaces, Skylids automatically open and close to bring in the sun's heat or shut cold out of a greenhouse. The architect designed the house for use in a temperate zone: not hot-dry climates such as Arizona, nor hot-wet areas such as Florida, but in most of the United States.

The four rooftop collectors have black-painted metal absorbers to collect the sun's heat, and glass sheets covering them trap most of the heat gained. Fan-forced air carries the heat through ducts to a basement rock storage area. From this storage area, hot air is circulated through the house. The passive part of the design makes up 500 square feet of greenhouse and sunroom space. These south-facing heat traps have openings to both the living room and the master bedroom (see plan, above) for heat gain and humidity and ventilation control. Two duct systems and two thermostats permit independent zoning of the greenhouse/sunroom/living room area and the rest of the house. A fifth collector, on the sunroom roof, sends heat to a basement water storage tank, preheating the domestic water supply. Conventional heating brings the water temperature up for washing needs, just as a conventional fossil-fuel system backs up the solar system for space heating. The fireplace, which also radiates heat, contains coils to supplement warming of the household hot water system.

For natural air flow cooling in summer, wide, paired louvers under the north roofs, opposite, vent out heat, summer hot air for syphonic cooling (see section, right). There are few windows on the north side of the house and high insulation standards are specified throughout the design. Insulating shutters are also provided for all the large window areas.

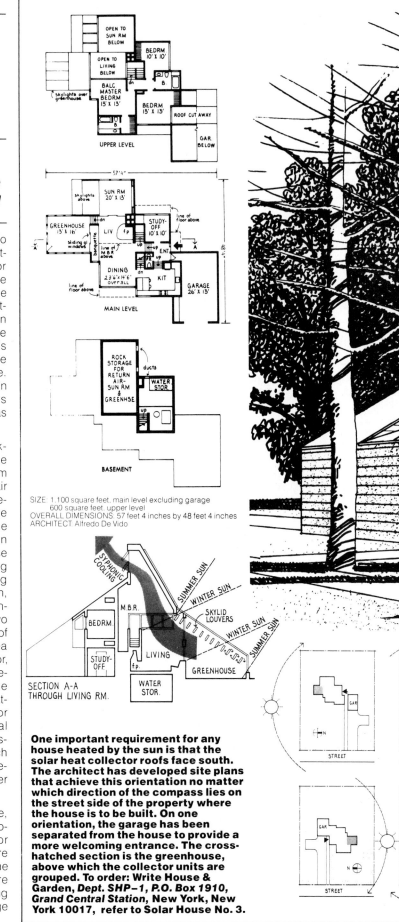

SIZE: 1,100 square feet, main level excluding garage
600 square feet, upper level
OVERALL DIMENSIONS: 57 feet 4 inches by 48 feet 4 inches
ARCHITECT: Alfredo De Vido

SECTION A-A THROUGH LIVING RM.

One important requirement for any house heated by the sun is that the solar heat collector roofs face south. The architect has developed site plans that achieve this orientation no matter which direction of the compass lies on the street side of the property where the house is to be built. On one orientation, the garage has been separated from the house to provide a more welcoming entrance. The cross-hatched section is the greenhouse, above which the collector units are grouped. To order: Write House & Garden, *Dept. SHP–1, P.O. Box 1910, Grand Central Station, New York, New York 10017,* refer to Solar House No. 3.

RENDERINGS: LEWIS BRYDEN

Solar house plan No. 4

Open to the south, protected on the north

Wise both to the sun and to family living needs, this two-story plan is both open and closed to provide privacy as well as energy requirements.

In its plan and its energy system, this house, designed by architect Robert P. Mocarsky for his own family, manages to be both open and closed, making the most of the attributes of each. On the south, the house is open and available to the sun with a 650-square-foot collector array on the roof. Also on this southern exposure, windows, doors, and porches connect the house to outdoor living where decks or patios can provide an easy transition from indoor to outdoor spaces. Inside, the main first-floor rooms — a sunken conversation and activity area, dining room and kitchen — also open internally to each other, sharing warmed air from the sunny south windows and exposed heating systems. In this partly two-story space, the solar energy system's pipes and ducts are exposed — with sun-warmed air circulated directly to the rooms or to an underground rock bin that holds the heat until it is needed.

The more closed part of the plan is designed to allow little of winter's coldest air inside, and to provide privacy for family members. The two-floor house has an insulated retaining wall and few large windows on the north, where laundry, powder room, activity area, den or bedroom range along the windowless insulated wall. To prevent cold air from entering major rooms, the entry is a vestibule on one side. A service entry also has two doors, with storage between. If a series of cold, cloudy days brings the thermostat too low, an electric backup system goes to work. For extra warmth a wood-burning stove is placed between the conversation and the dining areas. It's pipe is left exposed, as is the solar system ductwork, to radiate heat all the way up the two-story space. Upstairs, the master bedroom and children's rooms have a playroom in between.

When the architect built this house for his own family, a steep wooded site provided an opportunity to push the lower north side of the house into a bank to reduce heat loss. To see the house as he built it, see pages 76 and 77. To order this plan refer to Solar House No. 4.

UPPER LEVEL

LOWER LEVEL

SIZE: 1,500 square feet, first floor
1,100 square feet, second floor.
OVERALL DIMENSIONS: 58 feet 4 inches by 31 feet
ARCHITECT: Robert P. Mocarsky

RENDERING: LEWIS BRYDEN

Windows and overhangs, opposite, are designed so winter sun penetrates deep into the house, high summer sun does not. For natural air conditioning in summer, upper-level north windows let in coolest air; warm air rises and flows out high clerestory windows (see drawing, far right). Sections show exposed heating system's ductwork and the rock storage in the foundation level. The sloping shed roof accommodates 650 square feet of collector panels for space heating and domestic hot water requirements.

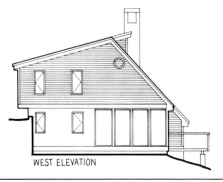

WEST ELEVATION

144

SOLAR
COLLECTORS

DUCT

DECK   STOVE   ACTIVITY

PLAY RM.

ROCK
BIN

SECTION A-A

SOLAR
COLLECTORS

DUCT

CL.   BATH

CONVERSATION   WORKSHOP

SECTION B-B

SUMMER SUN

WINTER SUN

NATURAL
COOLING

solar duct

SUMMER SUN

WINTER SUN

solar
duct

DINING

PLAYROOM

ACTIVITY

ROCK STORAGE

SECTION AA

Underground hybrid design utilizes solar power

Berms, passive and active solar technology, are combined in a striking house that works with nature to meet its energy needs.

An underground house of multi levels, designed by architect Alfredo De Vido, enjoys the earth's temperature-moderating advantages while gaining the light and energy of the sun through walls of south-facing windows and skylights. The house combines three energy-saving ideas: built-up earth berms or underground construction to shield the house from temperature fluctuations, a wall of glass for direct-gain passive solar heat, and collector arrays for both space heating and domestic hot water needs. Although solar collectors are specified in the plans for both space heating and domestic hot water, either or both could be deleted at the owner's option. The partially underground design would then rely only on its passive system for gathering the sun's energy. This is done through wall and roof areas of glass. Clerestory windows and skylights serve as a light scoop to brightly illuminate the living room from above and a reflective wall is provided that could further facilitate this reflection. The walls and floors are masonry, to provide thermal mass for the solar heat gain.

The heart of the house is the tiered garden room/dining area/living room which ascends up the hill for good functional reasons, but is also spatially interesting with sloping columns supporting the roof and a variety of ceiling heights. Adding additional interior design interest is the step-down pit around a heat circulating fireplace at the subterranean end of the living room. To avoid stratification of warm air in the high living space, a blow down duct is provided to recirculate warm air and provide good air distribution. Summer cooling is aided by operable skylights and a chimney effect from the natural flow of rising hot air. Operable insulating barriers also aid in controlling heat gain or loss at the extended glass areas. The bedrooms and kitchen areas also have levels stepped into the earth and are partially skylit and glazed to catch the sun. Half of each secondary bedroom is underground while the other half is glazed with skylights for solar gain, dividing the bedrooms into open and closed areas. An airlock is provided at the entry to the 3,100-square-foot house. To order this plan, refer to Solar House No. 5.

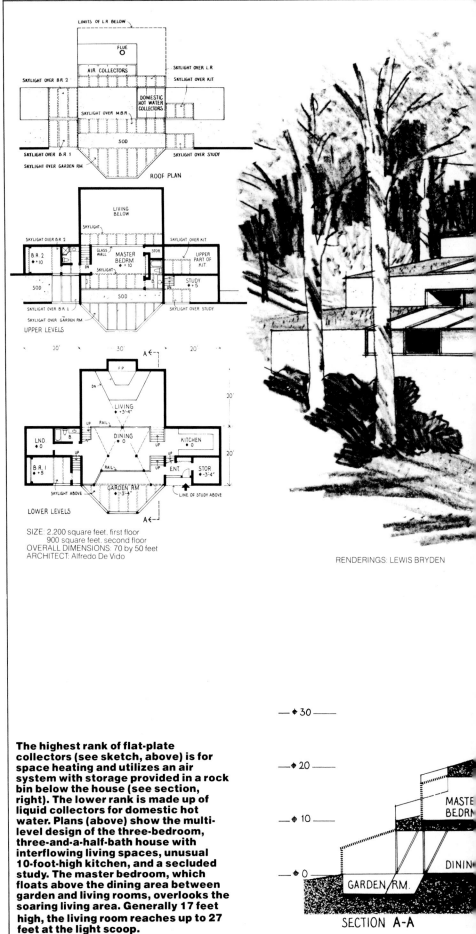

SIZE: 2,200 square feet, first floor
900 square feet, second floor
OVERALL DIMENSIONS: 70 by 50 feet
ARCHITECT: Alfredo De Vido

RENDERINGS: LEWIS BRYDEN

The highest rank of flat-plate collectors (see sketch, above) is for space heating and utilizes an air system with storage provided in a rock bin below the house (see section, right). The lower rank is made up of liquid collectors for domestic hot water. Plans (above) show the multi-level design of the three-bedroom, three-and-a-half-bath house with interflowing living spaces, unusual 10-foot-high kitchen, and a secluded study. The master bedroom, which floats above the dining area between garden and living rooms, overlooks the soaring living area. Generally 17 feet high, the living room reaches up to 27 feet at the light scoop.

LIVING

ROCK STORAGE

SOLAR:

Terms

Active solar systems use specialized hardware powered by some mechanical means to gather and carry heat to rooms or to storage until needed. Active components include fans, pumps, valves, thermostats. Also known as *indirect-gain* systems.

BTU (British Thermal Unit). The heat needed to raise one pound of water one degree Fahrenheit.

Collectors are the means for gathering (collecting) the sun's radiation. Although windows and walls can be collectors and often are in passive systems, the term usually refers to flat-plate collectors, which are the units on the roof or walls that catch solar heat in active solar systems. They are usually made up of metal absorber panels painted black and a heat transfer medium—air or water— that takes the heat from the absorber and distributes it to the point of use or storage. Glass or plastic covers the absorber to trap the heat gained.

Degree-days. The yearly total of daily temperatures below 65 degrees, used to calculate the heat loads for a particular climate.

Insolation. Spelled with an "o" instead of a "u," it means the amount of sun that strikes a given place, something the solar architect or designer needs to know to decide how much solar collector area will be required.

Passive solar systems are designed to utilize solar energy without mechanical hardware that requires electric power. Also known as *direct-gain* systems. Solar heat is caught through the design of the house, held and stored in the structure itself.

Retrofitting. Adapting existing structures for solar heat, now used to cover all those renovations that are done to save energy.

R-value. The amount of resistance insulation puts up to heat passing through it. The better the insulation, the higher the R-value. The R-value is usually printed on the material itself, or on the package.

Storage. Solar heating systems need a way to store heat overnight and for from one to five cloudy days. Plain water or rocks are the most common storage medium used. The water is stored in a large insulated tank, the rocks in a bin.

Solar electricity (photovoltaic). Photovoltaic cells are semiconductors that turn sunlight into electricity. All the satellites have been powered by photovoltaic cells, and so have many remote electrical installations on earth. Electricity from solar cells is still very, very expensive; but it has dropped in price from $200 per watt to less than $13 per watt in the last four years.

Economics

As 1976 drew to a close, the economic side of the solar energy picture took on a rosy glow as the Federal Energy Research and Development Administration (now the Department of Energy) released a study showing that solar heating could now compete economically with electricity in heating newly built, well-insulated, one-family houses in thirteen major cities across the United States.

The study, by the Metrek Division of the Mitre Corporation, covered Atlanta; Bismarck, North Dakota; Boston; Charleston, South Carolina; Columbia, Missouri; Dallas – Ft. Worth; Grand Junction, Colorado; Los Angeles; Madison, Wisconsin; Miami; New York City; Seattle; and Washington, D.C.

More specifically, the study commissioned by ERDA found solar energy could not only compete with electric heating in the major population centers throughout most of the United States, but also that if the cost of solar heating drops 25 percent from the present level, it would also then be competitive with fuel oil or electric heat pumps in many areas.

When the study was released, the director of the Federal Energy Research Agency's solar energy division said ERDA's goal would be "a 50 percent reduction in the cost of solar installations by 1980, through market competition, improved performance, reduced cost of equipment and installation, and possibly incentives. At that price," he said, "solar heating could be competitive with all fuels, including natural gas, in most regions of the country."

(The Mitre report, "An Economic Analysis of Solar Water and Space Heating," is available for $1.85. To get the report, write: Supt. of Documents, U.S. Government Printing Office, Washington, D.C. 20402. The identification number for the report is DSE-2333-1; the GPO stock number is 060-000-0038-7.)

In considering the costs of a solar system, Consumer Action Now's Council on Environmental Alternatives cautions against comparisons based on "first costs" alone, especially as fuel costs continue to increase. For that reason, the council suggests, it is advantageous to look at the cost of systems over their lifetime.

This method is known as life-cycle costing, in which the first cost of a solar system plus maintenance and financing costs over the lifetime of the system are compared to the first cost of a conventional heating system plus fuel, maintenance, and financing charges over the same lifetime.

Equipment

Estimates vary, but there are now some 600 manufacturers, both large and small, in the solar equipment business. The National Solar Heating and Cooling Information Center has compiled the names and addresses of manufacturers of solar equipment as well as lists of contractors, builders, and architects with solar energy experience.

The consumer's own inexperience and lack of knowledge in the field of solar energy, manufacturers who unintentionally build shoddy products and who are overenthusiastic about them, and deliberate fraud and misrepresentation are all obstacles that might have to be overcome in the solar marketplace.

By relying on competent engineering advice, many potential problems can be avoided, the National Solar Center advises, and gives advice on how to buy solar:

Ask for proof that the product will perform as advertised. The proof could come from an independent laboratory or a university. You should have the report itself, not what the manufacturer states the report claims.

Examine the warranty carefully. Remember that according to the law, the manufacturer must state that the warranty is full or limited. If it is limited, know what the limitations are. How long does the warranty last? Are parts, service, and labor covered? Who will provide the service? Does the equipment have to be sent back to the manufacturer for repairs? Make sure you understand the terms of the warranty before you buy. Ask the seller what financial arrangements, such as an escrow account, have been made to honor the warranties.

Solar components are like stereo components — some work well together, others don't. If the system you are purchasing is not sold as a single package by one manufacturer, be certain that the seller has strong experience in choosing compatible components.

Be sure you know specifically who will service the solar system if something goes wrong. Don't settle for a response like, "Any plumber or handyman will do."

Don't try a do-it-yourself kit unless you really have a very solid background as a handyman. One or two mistakes could make a system inoperable, and you will have no one to blame but yourself.

Don't forget your local consumer office or your Better Business Bureau. Both may be able to help you determine whether a seller is reputable or not. Check, too, to see whether there is a local volunteer citizens' solar organization around. If so, it can probably give you sound advice on solar applications in your area.

Information

The National Solar Heating and Cooling Information Center is a clearinghouse of solar energy information nationwide. Established by the Department of Housing (HUD), in cooperation with the Department of Energy (DOE), it has a mandate from Congress to collect, organize, and disseminate information about solar energy.

The center has put together computerized files on solar architects and builders, keeps lists of solar buildings, solar equipment manufacturers and distributors. It can supply information on solar economics, the latest solar legislation, and grants. The center also has its own engineering staff, which can be consulted, free of charge, on specific technical questions.

And it has a toll-free number that you can call for any of this information. The phone number is 800/523-2929, or 800/462-4983 in Pennsylvania. With questions of an involved nature, it is best to write: National Solar Heating and Cooling Information Center, PO Box 1607, Rockville, Maryland 20850.

Legislation

As the final segments of this book are being written it is the spring of 1978. The United States legislature has yet to enact the solar tax incentives proposed by President Carter in his first address to a joint session of Congress in April of 1977—over a year ago.

Designed to stimulate energy conservation and give impetus to solar energy, which the president described as "the most promising of new energy sources," the proposed federal tax credits may now be a temporary deterrent to the very goals the president set forth in his energy message. Although millions of Americans heard President Carter set a goal of using solar energy in more than 2½ million homes by 1985, they also heard tax incentives proposed to provide the initiative…and many may be waiting for that initiative to be forthcoming.

For some of us, the first page of the 1977 instructions from the Internal Revenue Service will serve as an ironic souvenir of the country's continuing inability to deal with the energy crisis. There it said: "At the time Form 1040 and these instructions were printed, Congress was considering legislation that would allow credits for energy-saving expenses for your personal residence. We have set aside line 45 and 61a…for these credits. If this legislation is passed…"

On a more positive note, it does appear that the solar proposals were the least controversial of the wide-ranging energy message's ambitious goals, and it is expected that the federal tax deductions for both energy conservation and retrofitting of existing buildings and the provision of solar heating systems in new buildings will soon be a plus factor in the growing solar house movement.

This is already widely true on the state level, where twenty-seven states have passed property tax incentives, and another twenty have legislation pending that will grant some sort of solar property tax relief.

Five years ago there was not a state law on the books in this country supporting solar energy for home heating or cooling. But in 1974, Indiana and Arizona enacted landmark legislation offering tax relief to homeowners who installed solar heating or hot water systems, and today there are more than thirty states with passed or proposed solar tax incentives.

These state and local tax incentives are important because they serve to encourage the purchase of solar systems as alternatives to more conventional energy sources; they can make solar construction easier by the alteration of building codes and zoning ordinances; and they can increase consumer confidence in solar equipment that has been monitored by state quality and performance regulations.

Twelve states have passed laws to safeguard a solar user's access to sunlight by various strategies, including the most common method of providing procedures for the creation of voluntary solar easements. Three states have altered building codes to encourage solar installations or design, and five have provided for solar equipment regulation.

Funds have also been provided for programs to promote solar research and development and some states have also required feasibility studies of alternative energy systems before beginning any substantial state construction. The first design award has just been given for a major solar building project in Sacramento, California, by that state government.

Most important, of course, is the fact that tax incentive legislation can reduce the initial costs of installing a solar system. This is done in states where income tax credits or deductions are allowed, usually for a given period of years after the house is built. In other states, sales tax exemptions for buyers or sellers of solar equipment are allowed. The chart on the following pages shows state solar legislation on tax incentives, solar access, building codes, and solar equipment standards regulation in effect as of December 1977. It was compiled by the National Solar Heating and Cooling Information Center, and information on the latest passed or proposed solar legislation may be obtained by writing to the center or calling its toll-free number, 800/523-2929, or 800/462-4983 in Pennsylvania.

STATE	BILL#	DESCRIPTION	CONTACT

I. Financial Incentives

STATE	BILL#	DESCRIPTION	CONTACT
Arizona	CH. 81 Laws of 1977	Provides income tax credit of 35% of cost of residential solar system up to $1000. Credit % declines 5% per year until program expires in 1984.	Director Dept. of Revenue Capitol Bldg., West Wing Phoenix, AZ 85017 (602) 271-3393
	CH.42 Laws of 1977	Exempts devices used for production of non-fossil energy from Transaction Privilege Sales Tax.	same as above
	CH. 93 Laws of 1975 as amended by CH. 129 Laws of 1976	Provides for amortization of the cost of solar energy devices over 36 months in computing net income for state income tax purposes. Applies to all types of buildings.	same as above
	CH. 165 Laws of 1974	Provides exemption from property tax increases which may result from addition of solar system to new or existing housing.	same as above
Arkansas	CH. 535 Laws of 1977	Allows individual homeowner taxpayer to deduct entire cost of energy saving equipment (including solar) from gross income for year of installation.	Dept. of Revenue Income Tax Section 7th & Wolfe Streets Little Rock, AR 72201 (501) 371-2193
California	CH. 168 Laws of 1976, as amended by CH. 1082 Laws of 1977	Provides for state income tax credit of 55% ($3000 maximum) of the cost of installing a solar system in a home. For any other building where the cost of the system exceeds $6000 the credit is the greater of $3000 or 25% of the system cost. Credit expires in 1981. Excess credit may be carried forward. Systems must meet criteria established by the Energy Resources Conservation Development Commission.	Franchise Tax Board P.O. Box 1468 Sacramento, CA 95807 (916) 355-0230
Colorado	CH. 344 Laws of 1975	Provides that all solar systems be assessed at 5% of their original value when computing property taxes.	Property Tax Administrator Division of Property Taxation 614 Capitol Annex Denver, CO 80203 (303) 892-2371
Connecticut	Public Act 457 (1977)	Provides sales and use tax exemptions for solar collectors.	State Tax Dept. Audit Division 92 Farmington Hartford, CT 06115 (203) 566-2501
	Public Act 409 (1976), as amended by Public Act 490 (1977)	Authorizes local taxing authorities to exempt property with solar system from increased assessment due to the system. Construction of solar portion must commence between October 1, 1976 and October 1, 1991. Exemption extends for 15 years after construction. Applies to new construction and retrofits.	Local Assessor or Board of Assessors.
Georgia	Act No. 1030 (1976)	Provides that purchasers of equipment for solar systems will receive refund of sales and use taxes paid on such equipment. Refund extends to July 1, 1986.	Department of Revenue Sales Tax Unit Room 310 Trinity—Washington Bldg. Atlanta, GA 30334 (404) 656-4071
	RES. No. 167 (1976)	Enabled constitutional amendment authorizing governing authority of any county or municipality to exempt the value of a solar system from *ad valorem* property taxation. Taxing authority must act before July 1, 1986.	Relevant City Council or County Board of Supervisors
Hawaii	Act 189 (1976)	Provides income tax credit for 10% of the cost of solar system for year of installation. System must be placed in service between December 31, 1975 and December 31, 1981. If credit exceeds tax liability, it can be carried forward to future years. Also provides exemption from any property tax increase resulting from the addition of a solar system. Exemption applies from June 30, 1976 through December 31, 1981.	Tax Department Ahle-Auhau Bldg. 425 Queen Street Honolulu, HI 96813 (808) 548-2211

STATE	BILL#	DESCRIPTION	CONTACT
Idaho	CH. 212 Laws of 1976	Provides that cost of residential solar systems may be deducted from taxable income over a period of four years. Deduction shall not exceed $5000 in any one taxable year.	Income Tax Division State Tax Commission P.O. Box 36 Boise, ID 83722 (202) 384-3290
Illinois	Public Act 79-943 (1975)	Provides that owner of a solar system installed on real property may claim improvement value of a conventional system if that value is less than value of solar system. System must conform to standards set by Illinois Division of Energy.	Division of Energy 222 South College Springfield, IL 62706 (217) 782-7500
Indiana	Public Law 15 (1974), as amended by Public Law 68 (1977)	Allows owner of real property with solar system an annual deduction from the assessed value of the property equal to the assessed value of the property with the solar system, minus the assessed value without the system. Also applies to mobile homes.	State Board of Tax Commissioners 201 State Office Bldg. Indianapolis, IN 46204 (317) 633-5358
Kansas	CH. 346 Laws of 1977	Allows business taxpayer to deduct amortized (60 months) cost of a solar system installed in a business or commercial building from taxable income. Can be applied in addition to the income tax credit provided by CH. 434 Laws of 1976.	Secretary of Revenue Second Floor, State Office Bldg. Topeka, KS 66612 (913) 296-3041
	CH. 345 Laws of 1977	Provides for reimbursement of 35% of *total* property tax paid for entire building or building addition if solar provides 70% of energy needed for heating or cooling of that building on an average annual basis.	same as above
	CH. 434 Laws of 1976	Allows individuals and businesses to deduct 25% of cost of solar system (up to $1000 for individuals and $3000 for businesses) from state income tax. System must be installed or acquired prior to July 1, 1983. Applies to taxable years after 1975.	same as above
Maine	CH. 542 Laws of 1977	Exempts solar heating systems from property taxation for five years from the date of installation. Exemption must be applied for. Also provides refund of sales or use tax paid on solar equipment certified as such by the Office of Energy Resources. Both tax provisions expire on January 1, 1983.	Local Assessor or Board of Assessors (For Property Tax) Office of Energy Resources 55 Capitol St. Augusta, ME 04330 (207) 289-2196 (For Sales Tax)
Maryland	CH. 740 Laws of 1976	Authorizes Baltimore City, any city within a county or any county to provide a credit against local real property taxes for those residential or non-residential buildings using solar heating or cooling units. Amounts and definitions are at the discretion of local jurisdiction.	Relevant City or County Department of Revenue
	CH. 509 Laws of 1975	Provides that a solar system shall not cause the property tax assessment of a new or existing building to be greater than it would be with a conventional system.	Department of Assessment & Taxation 301 W. Preston St. Baltimore, MD 21201 (301) 383-2526
Massachusetts	CH. 28 Laws of 1977	Authorizes banks and credit unions to make loans with extended maturation periods and increased maximum amounts for financing alternative energy systems including solar. Maturation period is extended to 10 years. Maximum amount is increased to $7000 for banks and $9500 for credit unions.	Local Bank or Credit Union
	CH. 487 Laws of 1976	Provides that a corporation may deduct the cost of a solar system from taxable income for year of installation. Also provides that the system will be subject to tangible property tax.	Commissioner of Corporations & Taxation 100 Cambridge St., Room 806 Boston, MA 02204 (617) 727-4201
	CH. 734 Laws of 1975	Provides for real estate tax exemption for solar system. Extends for 10 years after system installation.	Solar Action Office John McCormack State Office Bldg. One Ashburton Place Boston, MA 02108 (617) 727-7297

STATE	BILL#	DESCRIPTION	CONTACT
Michigan	Public Act 132 (1976)	Provides that receipts from sale of tangible property to be used in solar system shall not be used to compute tax liability for business activities tax.	Director Dept. of Treasury State Tax Commission State Capitol Bldg. Lansing, MI 48922 (517) 373-2910
	Public Act 133 (1976)	Provides that tangible property used for solar devices shall be exempt from excise (use) tax on personal property.	same as above
	Public Act 135 (1976)	Provides for exemption of solar devices from real and personal property taxes. Applicant for exemption must obtain exemption certificate from State Tax Commission. Commission's authority to issue certificate ends on June 30, 1985.	same as above
Montana	CH. 548 Laws of 1975	Allows property tax exemption on capital investments for energy conservation or alternative energy systems. Also allows public utility to lend capital for energy conservation/alternative energy systems at rate not exceeding 7% per year. Provides utilities with license tax credit for difference between 7% and prevailing rate of interest.	Director Dept. of Revenue Mitchell Building Helena, MT 59601 (406) 449-2460
	CH. 574 Laws of 1977	Provides solar income tax credit for residential solar energy system installed prior to December 31, 1982. Credit is for 10% of the first $1000 spent and 5% of the next $3000. If the federal government provides a similar tax credit, amount of credit is halved. If credit exceeds tax liability, it can be carried forward for up to four years.	Dept. of Revenue Income Tax Audit Section Mitchell Bldg. Helena, MT 59601 (406) 449-2837
Nevada	CH. 345 Laws of 1977	Provides property tax allowance for amount of assessed value of property with solar system minus assessed value without. Allowance may not exceed total value of property tax accrued or $2000, whichever is less.	Local County Assessor
New Hampshire	CH. 391 Laws of 1975, as amended by CH. 502 Laws of 1977	Allows each city and town to adopt (by local referendum) property tax exemptions for solar systems.	Local or Municipal Tax Assessor
New Jersey	CH. 256, Laws of 1977	Allows owner of real property with solar system annual deduction from property taxes equal to the remainder of assessed value of property with system minus assessed value without. Deduction must be applied for and expires on December 31, 1982. System must meet standards to be established by State Energy Office.	Director Division of Taxation West State and Willow Sts. Trenton, NJ 08625 (609) 292-5185
New Mexico	CH. 12 (Special Session of 1975), as amended by CH. 114 Laws of 1977	Provides income tax credit for 25% of cost of residential solar system. $1000 credit maximum. If credit exceeds tax liability, refund is paid. Also applies to solar powered irrigation and pumping equipment.	Bureau of Revenue Manuel Lujan, Sr., Bldg. St. Francis Drive at Alta Vista Santa Fe, NM 87503 (505) 837-3221
New York	CH. 322 Laws of 1977	Provides property tax exemption for solar and wind systems in amount of assessed value of property with system minus assessed value without. All exempted systems must be approved by state energy office. Exemption extends for fifteen years after approval. System must be installed prior to July 1, 1988.	Relevant Assessor or Board of Assessors
North Carolina	CH. 792 Laws of 1977	Allows personal and corporate income tax credit equal to 25% of the cost of the solar system installed in a building (limit $1000). System must meet performance criteria prescribed pursuant to the Solar Demonstration Act of 1974.	North Carolina Dept. of Revenue Individual Income Tax Div. P.O. Box 25000 Raleigh, NC 27640 (919) 733-4682
	CH. 965 Laws of 1977	Provides that buildings equipped with solar energy systems shall be assessed for property tax purposes as if they were equipped with a conventional system only. Becomes effective January 1, 1978 and expires December 1, 1985.	Local Assessor or Board of Assessors

STATE	BILL#	DESCRIPTION	CONTACT
North Dakota	CH. 537 Laws of 1977	Provides income tax credit for installation of solar or wind system equal to 5% a year for two years.	State Tax Department State Capitol Bismarck, ND 58505 (701) 224-3461
	CH. 508 Laws of 1975	Provides that solar heating or cooling systems used in new or existing buildings will be exempt from property taxes for five years following installation.	same as above
Oklahoma	H.B. 1322 (1977)	Provides income tax credit of 25% of the cost of a solar system installed in a private residence. Credit limitation is $2000. If allowance credit exceeds tax liability, the credit may be carried over for five succeeding taxable years. Credit expires on December 31, 1987.	Assistant Director, Income Tax Division N.C. Conners Bldg. 2501 Lincoln Blvd. Oklahoma City, OK 73194 (405) 521-3121
Oregon	CH. 196 Laws of 1977	Allows personal income tax credit of 25% ($1000 limit) of cost of installing alternative energy device (including solar) in a home. System must provide at least 10% of home's energy requirements and must meet performance criteria adopted by Department of Energy. Credit must be applied for and can be claimed for a device installed from January 1, 1978-January 1, 1985.	Oregon Department of Energy 528 Cottage, NE Salem, OR 97310 (503) 378-4040
	CH. 315 Laws of 1977	Permits veteran to obtain subsequent loan ($3000 limit) above the maximum amount allowed from Oregon War Veterans' Fund for the purpose of installing alternative energy device (including solar) in a home. System must meet performance criteria established by Director of Veterans' Affairs and Department of Energy, and must provide at least 10% of home's energy requirements.	Assistant Director Department of Veterans' Affairs 1225 Ferry St., SE Salem, OR 97310 (503) 378-6851
	CH. 460 Laws of 1975, as amended by CH. 196 Laws of 1977	Exempts property equipped with a solar system from *ad valorem* taxation in an amount equal to value of property with system minus value of property if it were not equipped with a solar system. Exemption is valid through December 31, 1997.	Administrator Assessment and Appraisal Division 506 State Office Building Salem, OR 97310 (503) 378-3378
South Dakota	CH. 111 Laws of 1975	Allows owners of residential real property an annual deduction from assessed value for installation of solar device. Deduction may be equal to the lesser of: (1) difference between assessed value with system and value without, or (2) $2000.	County Auditors/ Assessors and/or Secretary Department of Revenue State Capitol Pierre, SD 57501 (605) 224-3311
Texas	CH. 719 Laws of 1975	Provides exemption from sales taxes on receipts from sale, lease, and rental of solar devices. Business tax exemption granted to corporations which exclusively manufacture, install, and sell solar devices. Corporation may deduct amortized (60 months) cost of solar system from taxable capital.	Comptroller Director of Public Accounts LBJ Building 17th & Congress Austin, TX 78711 (512) 475-6001
Vermont	Public Law 226 (1976)	Allows town to enact real and personal property tax exemptions for solar systems.	State Energy Office State Office Building Montpelier, VT 05602 (802) 828-2768
Virginia	CH. 561 Laws of 1977	Allows county, city, or local governing body to exempt solar equipment from property taxation.	Relevant Tax Governing Body
Washington	CH. 364 Laws of 1977	Exempts solar energy systems from property taxation. Exemption must be applied for, is valid for seven years, and can only be applied to equipment meeting HUD's Minimum Property Standards. Opportunity to apply for exemption extends to December 31, 1981.	Director Property Tax Division Department of Revenue General Administration Building Olympia, WA 98504 (206) 753-2057

STATE	BILL#	DESCRIPTION	CONTACT

II. Solar Access

STATE	BILL#	DESCRIPTION	CONTACT
Colorado	**CH. 326 Laws of 1975**	Provides procedures for recording voluntary solar easements.	Relevant County Clerk or County Recorder
Kansas	**CH. 227 Laws of 1977**	Provides procedures for creation of voluntarily negotiated solar easements between property owners.	County Clerk or Recorder
Maryland	**CH. 934 Laws of 1977**	Provides that negotiated restrictions on the use of land or water for the purpose of protecting solar access shall be enforceable in law and equity. Restrictions can be created by voluntarily negotiated easements, covenants, restrictions, or conditions between property owners.	Relevant Clerk or Recorder
New Mexico	**CH. 169 Laws of 1977**	Declares that access to sunlight is a transferable property right. Provides that disputes over solar access shall be resolved by prior appropriation rule modified by court decisions. Effective 7/1/78.	City or County Zoning Authority
North Dakota	**CH. 425 Laws of 1977**	Provides procedures for the creation of voluntary solar easements.	Relevant Clerk or Recorder
Oregon	**CH. 153 Laws of 1975**	Adds solar energy considerations to comprehensive planning. Allows city and county planning commissioners to recommend ordinances governing building height for solar purposes.	Director Dept. of Energy 528 Cottage Street N.E. Salem, OR 97310 (503) 378-4128

III. Standards for Solar Systems

STATE	BILL#	DESCRIPTION	CONTACT
Connecticut	**Public Act 409 (1976)**	Provides that Commissioner of Planning and Energy Policy establish standards for solar energy systems sold in state.	Dept. of Planning and Energy Policy 20 Grant St. Hartford, CT 06115 (203) 566-2800
Florida	**CH. 246 Laws of 1976**	Directs Florida Solar Energy Center to develop standards for solar systems sold in state and testing procedures to evaluate them. All solar systems manufactured or sold in the state may optionally display results of approved performance tests.	Florida Solar Energy Center 300 State Road 401 Cape Canaveral, FL 32920 (305) 783-0300
Minnesota	**CH. 333 Laws of 1976**	Directs building code division of Department of Administration to develop performance criteria for solar systems made or sold in-state. These standards must be in reasonable conformance with Federal Interim Performance criteria for residential and commercial solar systems. Manufacturers and retailers are required to disclose the extent to which each system meets these standards.	Building Code Division Department of Administration Seventh & Roberts Sts. St. Paul MN 55101 (612) 296-4626

IV. Building Code Provisions

STATE	BILL#	DESCRIPTION	CONTACT
California	**CH. 670 Laws of 1976**	Provides that any city or county may require new buildings subject to state housing law to be constructed so as to permit the future installation of solar devices. Specific building features mentioned include roof pitches and alignments.	Division of Codes & Standards Department of Housing & Community Development 921 10th Street Sacramento, CA 95814 (916) 445-9471
Florida	**CH. 361 Laws of 1974**	Provides that no single family residence shall be constructed in the state unless the plumbing is designed to facilitate future installation of solar water heating equipment.	Bureau of Codes and Standards 2571 Executive Center Circle East Tallahassee, FL 32301

Insulation

Anyone serious about utilizing solar energy also has to be serious about energy conservation, which in building comes down to insulation. Because solar heat is quickly dissipated by a drafty, thin-walled house, all agree on the importance of insulation, caulking, weather-stripping, double-glazing, shuttering, and any other way of sealing up heated space. This can cut heating demand by as much as 50 percent, a plus whatever heat system is used.

Experts now recommend more than doubling what used to be normal insulating patterns. Insulation is measured in R-value, the amount of resistance a material puts up to heat passing through it. The higher the R-value, the better the insulation. The R-value is usually printed on the material itself, or on the package of insulating material.

The amount of insulation required depends on the climate where a house is being built. In a recent government publication, the U.S. Department of Energy gives recommended R-values for ceilings, walls, and floors in five climate zones (see chart below). The climates were measured by degree-days and plotted on a map of the United States. Increasingly, it is understood that solar designing has to take in the factors of these given climate zones just as insulation does.

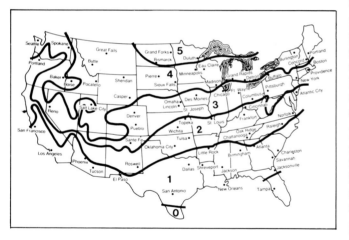

R-value for:	Zone 1	Zone 2	Zone 3	Zone 4	Zone5
Ceilings	R-26	R-26	R-30	R-33	R-38
Walls	R-13	R-19	R-19	R-19	R-19
Floors	R-11	R-13	R-19	R-22	R-22

Insulation itself is simply building material that has many pockets of trapped air distributed through its thickness that resist the passage of heat. To understand why this is important, it is necessary to understand that heat always moves from a warmer object or area to a colder one; it wants to even itself out or find a uniform level like water or air.

This natural movement of heat from warmer to colder surfaces and volumes is related to their differences in temperature. When the indoor and outdoor temperatures are within 20 degrees of each other, the intensity of heat transfer is negligible. But when the difference climbs to 60 or 70 degrees, heat from inside virtually flies through the walls and roof of uninsulated houses. The same transfer takes place in reverse in summer, when the sun beats down on the roof all day. So insulation works both ways.

To move through a wall, heat is conducted through the solid material (such as the inner surface of plaster or gypsum board). It flows easily from molecule to molecule of such materials toward the cold. But when it comes to an air pocket, it must change into radiant heat to cross that space. That slows it down, because less heat can be transferred by radiation than by conductance. When the heat hits the other side of the air pocket, it must turn back into conducted heat. And so on. The more separate air spaces, the better.

For this reason, wood is an excellent natural insulator—its interlocking microscopic fibers have lots of air around them. The insulating materials available and used today—foamed plastics, glass fiber, mineral wood, and a variety of fiberboards — all have a capacity similar to wood. They resist the passage of heat, but at much cheaper cost.

Most of our houses, even many that appear to be built of brick or stone, have wood-frame construction. That means the walls are essentially hollow — a 3- or 4-inch-wide gap with more than a foot of space between each upright member or stud. The roof and top floor ceiling, likewise, generally have more than a foot of space between the rafters and joists. Those spaces are perfect for insulation.

Heat loss varies through the roof, walls, and floors. The roof is the most vulnerable, because warm air rises. The thickest layer of insulation (see chart) must go there, either in the roof structure or in the floor of an attic. Exterior walls are the next most important, and, finally, floors over unheated or exposed areas.

In addition to roofs, walls, and floors, windows and doors also have to be insulated. This is important because windows account for most heat loss in a house. In an average dwelling, 10 to 13 percent of the area is glass, but 50 percent of the total heat loss is through that area.

The reason is simple: Where an insulated wall may have a value of R-3 or more, a single glass window is only R-.88. Insulating windows — two panes of glass sealed into the sash with an air space between them—can cut heat losses in half. Separate storm windows do a little better than that, because of the greater air space between the panes of glass. Double-paned windows plus storm windows — triple-glazing—cut heat losses by two-thirds.

And so, double-paned windows are essential in energy-conscious houses—plus storm windows and/or insulating shutters on the inside where possible. Weather stripping, storm doors, and air-lock entries also cut down on air infiltration.

Landscaping

There is nothing like a shade tree to help cool a house in the summer and allow sun to warm rooms in winter. A deciduous tree—one that sheds its leaves in the fall—is best for this purpose. Bare branches allow free passage for low-angled rays of the winter sun, with a definite fuel-saving effect in whichever room the solar rays penetrate. In the summer, when those rays can provide more heat than is desirable, a deciduous tree's leaves are in bloom to serve as nature's own sun screen.

A single shade tree, strategically placed on the south or west side of the house, can equal the cooling effect of a sizable power-driven air conditioner — without its noise. Not only does the tree shade the roof, windows, and outdoor sitting area, on sunny days it actually creates its own breeze.

In locating shade trees, it should be remembered that the hottest summer sunshine comes in the afternoon when the sun moves into the northwest part of the sky. There should be at least 20 feet of clearance allowed between the tree trunk and any part of a building, more than that for trees with potentially wide-spreading branches, like beech. Tree branches should never scrape against shingles or siding, and dense foliage right up against a window can impede air circulation instead of helping it.

Evergreens can also play a part in conserving energy. A windbreak of pine, hemlock, or arborvitae on the side of the house toward prevailing winter winds can be a definite help in cutting fuel consumption. A double or triple row of trees is much more effective than a single row, and the plants should be close enough together to form a solid mass after a few years of growth. Windbreak plantings, however, should not be close enough to the house to stop summertime breezes or clog gutters and downspouts with falling needles.

Foundation plantings are another way to protect a house in cold weather. The joint where the foundation and house siding meet can be particularly vulnerable to cold air. An evergreen foundation planting can help keep cold air away from this weak spot.

Spreading yew is effective in this location, and mountain laurel and rhododendrons can perform equally well. Plants should be kept within bounds, though, and not permitted to grow tall enough to cut off light and air from windows.

A side benefit of all kinds of trees: Their dead branches or prunings, as well as any trees cut for thinning purposes, make excellent fuel for fireplaces and wood stoves.

Following is a list of the top six shade trees for most parts of the United States:

1. European beech, *Fagus sylvatica*. A magnificent, long-lived, very large — eventually — and generally pest-free European tree that has been grown in this country for generations. The purple- and copper-leaved varieties are particularly beautiful, but the plain green species is just as good for shade.

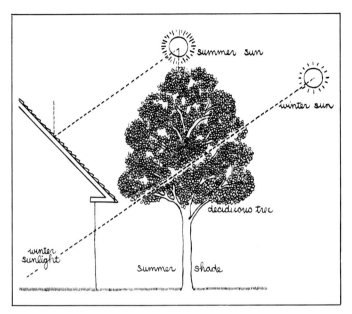

2. Little-leaf linden, *Tilia cordata*. A common street tree in Europe, this linden, sometimes called lime tree, has flowers with a delightful perfume in midsummer. The top is dense and very symmetrical, making it particularly good for shading a patio or terrace.

3. Pin oak, *Quercus palustris*. A straight, upright trunk and spreading horizontal branches make this American native an ideal shade tree. Hardy everywhere and resistant to extremes of dryness and wetness, it is also one of the few oaks with handsome fall coloring. Pin oak is also resistant to wind damage and drops very little in the way of litter.

4. Willow oak, *Quercus phellos*. Narrow, willowlike leaves give this native of the southeastern states its name. The horizontally branched, symmetrical top casts a fine shade all summer long. However, it is not reliably hardy north of the latitude of New York City.

5. Sweet gum, *Liquidambar styraciflua*. This native of the eastern coastal region has interesting, star-shaped leaves and a rather irregular but wide-spreading top. A fresh, light green all summer, the leaves turn beautifully varied shades of yellow, red, and purple in the fall. A possible objection to sweet gum is the spiny seed cluster, which can be decidedly uncomfortable when stepped on by a bare foot. It is hardy as far north as Boston and seems to thrive in either dry or swampy ground.

6. Sugar maple, *Acer saccharum*. Best known as the source of maple syrup, sugar maple is one of the finest of all North American trees. The top is rather open, but leafy enough to give really effective shade. Fall color may be either red or yellow—each is truly spectacular. Hardy well into Canada, sugar maple is easy to transplant and not particular about soil or location. West of the Mississippi, the native black maple, *Acernigrum*, is very similar and may be used in the same way.

Bibliography

Solar books, booklets,
catalogs, journals, kits,
magazines, research papers

Bruce Anderson
Solar Energy: Fundamentals in Building Design
McGraw-Hill, New York, New York 10020
$21.50

Bruce Anderson, with Michael Riordan
The Solar Home Book
Brick House Publishing Company, Church Hill,
Harrisville, New Hampshire 03450
$7.50

Steve Baer
Sunspots: Collected Facts and Solar Fiction
(expanded second edition)
Zomeworks, Box 712, Albuquerque, New Mexico 87103
$4.00

Farrington Daniels
Direct Use of the Sun's Energy
First published in 1964, reissued 10 years later
in a new edition; Ballantine Books, New York,
New York 10022
$1.95

Eugene Eccli
*Low-Cost, Energy Efficient Shelter: For the Owner
and Builder*
Rodale Press, Inc., Emmaus, Pennsylvania 18049
$10.95; $5.95 paperback

Rick Fisher and Bill Yanda
The Food and Heat Producing Solar Greenhouse
John Muir Press, P.O. Box 613, Santa Fe,
New Mexico 87501
$6.50

**Jim Lecki, Gil Masters, Harry Whitehouse,
Lily Young**
Other Homes and Garbage
Sierra Club Books, San Francisco, California 94108
$9.95

James C. McCullagh
The Solar Greenhouse Book
Rodale Press, Inc., Emmaus, Pennsylvania 18049
$10.95; $8.95 paperback

Richard Merrill and Thomas Gage
Energy Primer, Solar, Water, Wind and Biofuels
Dell Publishing Company, Inc.,
New York, New York 10017
$7.95

**Dan Scully, Don Prowler, Bruce Anderson,
with Doug Mahone**
*The Fuel Savers, a Kit of Solar Ideas for Existing
Homes*
Total Environmental Action, Inc., Church Hill,
Harrisville, New Hampshire 03450
$2.75

W. A. Shurcliff
Solar Heated Buildings of North America
Brick House Publishing Company, Church Hill, Harrisville,
New Hampshire 03450
$12.00

Norma Skurka and Jon Naar
Design for a Limited Planet, Living with Natural Energy
McGraw-Hill, New York, New York 10020
$12.95; $5.95 paperback (Ballantine Books)

Alex Wade and Neal Ewenstein
30 Energy-Efficient Houses You Can Build
Rodale Press, Inc., Emmaus, Pennsylvania 18049
$10.95; $8.95 paperback

Donald Watson
*Designing & Building A Solar House: Your Place in
the Sun*
Garden Way Publishing, Charlotte, Vermont 05445
$8.95

Malcolm Wells and Irwin Spetgang
How to Buy Solar Heating — Without Getting Burnt
Rodale Press, Inc., Emmaus, Pennsylvania 18049
$6.95 Paperback

Solar Dwelling Design Concepts
U.S. Department of Housing & Urban Development,
Superintendent of Documents, U.S. Government
Printing Office, Washington, D.C. 20402
Prepared by AIA Research Corporation $2.30

Solar-Oriented Architecture
AIA Research Corporation, 1735 New York Avenue,
N.W., Washington, D.C. 20006
*Prepared by Arizona State University College of
Architecture* $15.00

Catalog of Solar Industries
The Solar Energy Industries Association,
1001 Connecticut Avenue, N.W., Suite 632,
Washington D.C. 20036 $8.00

In the Bank...Or Up the Chimney?
Superintendent of Documents, U.S. Government
Printing Office, Washington, D.C. 20402 $1.70

Making the Most of Your Energy Dollars
Superintendent of Documents, U.S. Government
Printing Office, Washington, D.C. 20402 $.70

The Solar Age Catalog
Cheshire Books, Harrisville, New Hampshire 03450 $8.50

Solar Age Magazine
Solar-Vision, Inc., 212 East Main Street, Port Jervis
New York 12771 $20 a year

Solar Energy and Your Home
National Solar Heating and Cooling Information
Center, P.O. Box 1607, Rockville, Maryland 20850 free

Solar Energy Books
National Solar Energy Education Campaign, 10762
Tucker Street, Beltsville, Maryland 20705 $4.50

Solar Energy Digest
P.O. Box 17776, San Diego, California 92117
$28.50 a year

Index

Architects, solar
consultants,
designers, equipment
manufacturers, and
photographers